Get Out of Your Boxx!

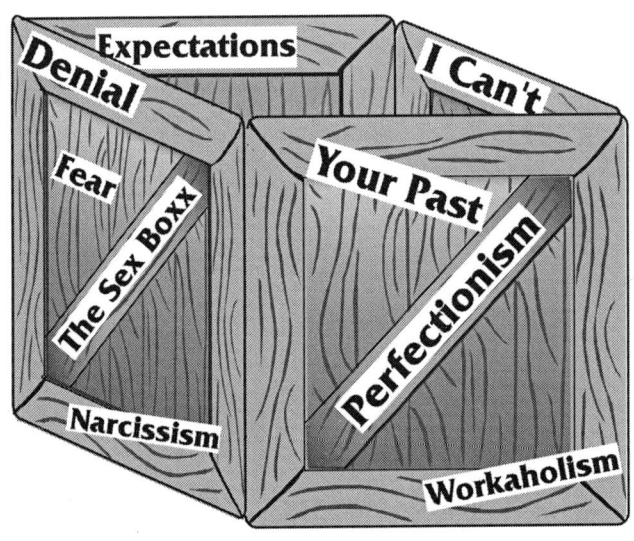

GET OUT OF YOUR BOXX!

AND LIVE THE LIFE YOU REALLY WANT...

But First Don't Forget to Drive the Carpool, Call Your Client, and Make Love to Your Spouse!

Mary Jo Fay

Illustrated by Janice Green

Out of the Boxx, Inc.
Parker, Colorado

Copyright © 2003 by Mary Jo Fay

All rights reserved, including the right of reproduction in whole or in part in any form without written permission from the author except in the case of brief quotations embodied in critical articles and reviews. No liability is assumed for damages that may result from the use of information within this book.

For more information contact www.outoftheboxx.com

Cover design by Janice Green
Back cover photo by Barb Walker

Printed in the United States of America

ISBN 0-9743504-6-X
Library of Congress Control Number 2003095313

OUT of the BOX
inc.

To Mom - for understanding.
To Dad - for teaching me to ride.
To Shaun - for being incredible.
and
To Barb and Sara, the most awesome cheerleaders I've ever had!

Acknowledgements

There are so many people who have helped me along this book's journey. It has been a labor of love … not just my own labor, but that of many others whose love and support has shown through each and every step of the way.

The biggest thanks go to my sister Barb Walker and my friend, Sara Coley. What started out as a "Success Team" nearly seven years ago, has become the strongest network of cheerleaders, supporters, and incredible women I have ever known. Their time reading and editing this book was over and above the call of duty. Their suggestions and critiques helped make it what it is. Their ongoing belief in me and support during some dark times in my life have gotten me where I am today. I owe them everything.

To my awesome daughter, Shaun, I give thanks for her understanding of my journey. In addition, her sensitivity and insight regarding some of my early columns gave me a new approach, which runs throughout this book. ("Quit preaching to others Mom, and proclaim your own stuff as well!") I am so proud of her! She has been my best friend for many years and that gift has helped me through many difficult times. It is such a pleasure now to watch her on her own journey.

My mom has been incredible as she has learned to understand my mission and respect the path I have chosen. It has been a learning process for both of us, and I want to thank her from the bottom of my heart for her support. I know how difficult it was at times.

Then, there were the variety of movers and shakers: Janice Green who provided the fabulous artwork and had unending patience with me. Joe Sabah, who gave me a swift kick in the butt to get this project off the ground in the first place.

Steve Eldridge of the *Denver Nursing Star* for providing me with my first writing outlet. Scott Laudenslager, of Kimco printing for his support and technical pieces of information that sent me in the right direction. And to all the readers who gave me input, commentary and editorializing. Thanks to all of you.

There were many emotional supporters too: Kris Garrett was an angel of support. My incredible friend Jose Juan Azpiazu helped me find the courage to believe in myself. Scott Olsen listened and shared his questions and philosophy with me for hours on end. Thanks for being my guinea pig! And Sheila Martin for giving me my first speaking opportunity as well as for being an intense reviewer and a great friend.

Special thanks to Sam Vaknin and Marilyn Van Derber, whose books were incredibly valuable to me personally. Hopefully with their insights, my writing will also help educate others to the dangers of living with narcissism and sexual abuse.

And to my dog Asher, who kept me company during many hours of writing. His need for regular attention and a quick round of fetch helped get my brain recharged whenever I hit a slow spot. His unconditional love and sensitivity was irreplaceable. He is my greatest fan.

To Dr. Joe, Rangel, Sand Dollar Sports and all my other supporters in Mexico who helped me through some tough times. And to all the people who believed in my mission and never let me slack off – thank you to all of you.

But mostly, to so many people who shared their personal stories with me, I will be forever in your debt. Without you, this book would not exist. Your candor and openness led me down paths I never dreamed of. Hopefully, from your stories of pain and success, others will grow as well.

And to all of you who have already contacted me telling me that I have made a difference – you will never know what that means to me. My mission meant something …

Contents

Part One
The Road To Discovery 1
1. Running Away From Home 3
2. Rediscovering The World Of Possibilities 14
3. What Boxx? 19

Part Two
Identifying Your Boxxes 27
4. Fear: The Biggest Boxx Of All 28
5. "I Can't, I Should, I Have To!" 39
6. Boxxed In By Your Past 53
7. The Oh-So-Perfect Boxx 64
8. Workaholism And The Wrong Career —
   The Treadmill Boxxes 72
9. A Weighty Boxx 86
10. The Unfulfilling Empty Boxx 96
11. The Sex Boxx –
    The Good, The Bad, And The Ugly 106
12. Deadly, Secret Boxxes 122
13. So Many Boxxes, So Little Time 133
14. Are You Boxxing With Denial? 145

Part Three
Trapped By Someone Else's Boxx 152

    15. The Expectations Of Others 153

    16. Narcissism — Boxxed In By
        The "Master Of The Universe".......................164

Part Four
Breaking Down The Walls 175

    17. The Investigation Leads To 176

    18. If Not Now, When ? 189

    19. Your Plan of Attack! 199

    20. Your Powerful Weapons...............................219

    21. Sabotage or Success? 237

    22. It's Your Journey … 247

    More Out Of The Boxx Possibilities 252

What is a Boxx?

Different than a regular box a "Boxx" is a behavioral pattern that holds its captive hostage, limiting the view of life's possibilities, excitements, and passions!

"Today is the first day of the BEST of your life!"   *Barb Walker*

Part One
The Road To Discovery

*E*ver feel like you're "Stuck in a Boxx?" Caught on an endless treadmill? Life's ups and downs, combined with the daily stress of the "speed of light" pace of our American culture can leave people feeling as if they live inside a tornado each and every day! Keeping up with kids, job, relationships, courtship and love, responsibilities, bill paying, time constraints, and Little League practice can leave most of us exhausted, frustrated, and downright frazzled! Who has time for taking care of yourself when there doesn't even seem to be time to breathe?!

That was me. Overstressed. Overtaxed. Overwhelmed. Over the edge! I was caught in a frantic maze called life and didn't know how to survive, until I got Out of My Boxx! This is the story of my journey and the discoveries I uncovered along the way. One of the most important lessons I learned was that the road to self-discovery frequently proves to be a wild ride, and mine was no exception! I hope by sharing my story with you that you might find some nuggets of information to spark a flame in you on your own journey; that you too can find more excitement, more fun, more satisfaction, and more pure passion in your life than you ever dreamed possible! And that you can find it without weathering some of the storms I did!

So, if you can slow your life down long enough to pass on the carpool this once, return your client's phone calls later,

Get Out of Your Boxx

and tell your sweetheart you'll make love in just a little while, you might find a spark somewhere in these pages that can make your small flame explode into fireworks that can change your life! Get off your treadmill! Get Out of Your Boxx! Figure out how to do it and still juggle all those things you do, because they're not going away anytime soon!

If you're still convinced you don't have time, then let me ask you this: If not now, when? Ten years from now, if you're still living on the treadmill, frantically running like a crazed hamster, how will you feel? If ten years from now you still haven't taken the time to take care of yourself, how frustrated will you be? Ten years from now, will you ask yourself why you wasted so much time doing the "same old, same old" stuff everyday? Why you didn't spend your life doing the things you REALLY wanted to do? So, I ask you again. If not now, when? When is it time to take care of YOU first, for a change?

My journey taught me that the time is now! Each day is a gift! To waste even one is a terrible loss. But I had to learn all these lessons the hard way. So, hang onto your seats, as the road is bumpy and starts out in a pit of despair that seems without escape. I assure you, it has a happy ending!

"Life is either a daring adventure or nothing."
Helen Keller

Chapter 1
Running Away From Home

As I look back upon everything now, it all makes so much more sense. Yet, at the time I was writing my own suicide letter it seemed hopeless, deafeningly silent, endlessly painful, and without reason. A deep, dark, void where I was suspended in chronic confusion and self-doubt, and cloaked in a blanket of not feeling valuable to anyone in my life.

The depression I had fought for months had taken its toll on me. It had worn me down for a very long time, little by little, without me even realizing it. Then, when even bigger life events came along, the straws began to break the camel's back, although they seemed more like logs than straws at the time — and they came in multiples.

First of all, I had been in marriage counseling with my husband for four, long years. (That, in itself, would leave most struggling for some sense of stability and security.) Secondly, at the beginning of September, I had sent my only child off to college. Third, only days after that, the tragedies of September 11 hit every person in this country, unlike anything we had ever seen. Fourth, to top everything off, after planning to file for divorce for several weeks, I finally took that tentative but necessary step, on October 5. I held my breath, hoping that I was making the right decision.

The result? By November, there was little left of me. Predictably, the stress only continued to mount with the added strain of a relationship in transition. Walking away from a 23-year marriage was not done lightly, nor without guilt, baggage, and second thoughts.

Yet, perhaps the most profound shock of the enormous pile of "stuff" I was juggling was that when my daughter left for college I lost my best friend, and at a time when I was in the lowest place in my life. I never realized that her leaving and cutting the "apron strings," would hit me so hard. Although she was still geographically nearby, I felt the additional distance of the typical "independence dance" that occurs between teenagers and their parents. It left me feeling rebuffed, irrational, and incompetent.

The words I wrote in that suicide letter were horrible. Words that were meant not only to wound, but to leave life-long scars and vivid memories. My heart was so shredded that I couldn't think of anyone else at that point — only the extreme pain that I was carrying inside me. Pain from years of unhappiness. Of not feeling loved. Of feeling worthless and empty. Of striving to do my best but just never quite feeling like I could do anything right. Or that what I did do never mattered to anyone. This, in spite of life-long accomplishments too numerous to mention.

Tears streamed down my face and gut-wrenching sobs filled me as I wrote words that I knew would hurt everyone I loved. I had held in my anger and my pain for so long that it came in a tidal wave more powerful than I could control. My hands almost felt possessed as I kept pouring out my feelings on the keyboard, advising the survivors which music to play at my funeral … "Why Have You Gotta Be Angry All the Time," by Tim McGraw, and "I Learned That From You," by Sara Evans. They felt like my theme songs. I wanted everyone at my funeral to understand their messages.

I kept debating on the method to take my own life. I felt so vengeful that I wanted to make as big a statement as possible. I had always thought that carbon monoxide would be the most "civil" route available and wouldn't leave much of a mess for anyone to clean up. (There I was, worrying about everyone else first again!) But at that moment, I highly considered sitting in the middle of the kitchen floor and slitting my wrists and letting my blood color everything ... leaving a huge mess for someone to clean up. It just seemed a powerful, final statement. As a friend of mine commented later, "the overwhelming act of revenge." It seemed fitting.

Yet, somehow in those moments of tears, pain, sobs, and depression, a little voice in me begged for life. Begged me not to quit. Pleaded with me to let the love for my child win out over the pain in my heart. She should not have to carry that monumental burden with her for the rest of her life. It was more than anyone should have to bear — no matter how terrible I felt. What she had never truly understood was how many times she had already saved my life over the years during my intermittent battles with depression. I had considered suicide on many occasions, but knowing I would be leaving a young child without a mother was the strongest lifeline that she could have given me.

Suddenly, my sobs turned into screams as I realized that I must continue living. I cried out at the top of my lungs in the middle of the night — although no one heard me except God and the dog.

I really don't know how the next steps happened. I just suddenly knew I needed to make some kind of serious change or I would only return to this spot sometime in the future – it was only a matter of time. Whether I would actually take my own life, or be in such an oblivious state of mind that I drove headlong into traffic, or simply curled up and died of depression, I didn't know. What I did know was that I must do something different immediately or I would be dead within a handful of months, at the rate I was going.

So how did I change my life? What happened to change my path after I wrote that suicide letter?

Get Out of Your Boxx

Well, I started listening to my heart and being true to MYSELF, first and foremost. I realized I had been living in some very confining, claustrophobic, high expectation "boxxes" and it had been slowly killing me. I had defined myself by my roles, my job, my volunteer work, my marriage, my daughter, my horses, my truck, and even my house and miscellaneous possessions. I had been doing things for everybody else in hopes that it would make others love me more when, in fact, I hadn't been true to ME first. I just hadn't realized that yet. And so – I decided to Get Out of My Boxx! I don't think I actually knew any of that at the time — it was simply a "knee-jerk response." My "fight or flight" mechanism kicked into gear, as it often did. Yet, this time it said something different than usual. It said, "Go far away ... go VERY far away." The actual lessons of the boxxes developed over a much longer time.

I tell people that I "ran away from home." I guess I felt that since I never did that as a child, I was fully entitled to do so as a grown-up. My daughter was in college so I was past the responsibility of daily mothering. I had already filed for divorce and therefore had no one to be accountable to at home. I realized just how tired I was of living in a relationship where I felt empty and unfulfilled. My part-time job I knew I could replace with another elsewhere. It occurred to me that all those pieces had fallen into place for a reason and I recognized that it was time I became responsible for taking care of ME. I HAD to put me first. Immediately. Before it was too late.

Fortunately, I was blessed with some good friends who recognized the seriousness of my depression although I don't think even they knew how truly "on the brink" I was. They asked me if I had a credit card, if I had any "room" on it, and if I wouldn't like to go somewhere for a while. After saying yes to all of the above, they asked me where I would like to go for a week and as it was November in Colorado, I answered, "somewhere warm where I can scuba dive."

The end result was that I went on a week-long vacation to Cozumel, Mexico. By myself. Alone. Mind you, I had traveled by myself dozens of times before on business. Yet, this trip was different. This one was with a new definition to begin with – I was *not* on business, but on vacation. A single woman on vacation *By Herself!* The entire concept felt very weird. What would people say? I didn't know whether to be excited, or nervous, or worried about what "everyone else would think."

The weight of stress which I carried like an anvil around my neck immediately lifted upon arriving in that wonderful, tropical paradise with its sunshine, surf, and sea. I suddenly felt like I was being swaddled in a warm blanket on a freezing, cold night. This haven not only provided life sustaining warmth but that special comfort of snuggling down and feeling safe. Even though on one hand, I was this person who was an incredible bundle of nerves, at the same time I felt like someone incognito. Someone on a secret mission. Someone who no one knew. Someone who could be who I wanted to be without needing anyone else's permission or acceptance. There was no one there to tell me I should or shouldn't do this or that. It was like being reborn. Ironically, it was Thanksgiving Day, 2001. If that wasn't an omen from God, then I didn't know what was!

I found an incredible peace in Cozumel that gave me hope. Actually, I suddenly felt a closeness to God that I had never experienced in my life. My first night there, I sat all alone on the beach at midnight. The stars were crystal clear. The moon was full. The sound of the gentle waves lapping at the sand at my feet was almost deafeningly quiet. And in that quiet, I truly had an epiphany.

It's probably important to note here, that before this time, God and I weren't on the greatest of terms. Yes, I believed in God and had been indoctrinated in all the church functions growing up, but I guess I had "blamed" God for some bad things that had happened in my life and I hadn't really gone out of my way to be friends with him.

In that moment on the beach, I was knocked over by the most gentle, but powerful of messages. I truly believe that God said to me,

"OK, Mary Jo. You know that story of how God only gives you as much as you can carry? Well, I realize that I pushed you right to the edge of that limit, but you passed the test with flying colors! I know you wonder why your life has been so hard for a while. Well, first of all, I really needed you and your husband to come together to create your daughter. I have a special job for her and I needed the qualities that both of you brought to the table to make her into the beautiful person that she is, and I needed you to raise her to adulthood. Now it's time for her to be on her own path and it's your time to take care of you. And by the way, when you're done with that – and feel free to take whatever time you need – I have a special job for you too."

I felt a relief like I have never felt in my life. The incredible message that came loud and clear to me gave me a new strength. A strength which helped me start to know the answers. I let go of so much "stuff" I had carried around that wasn't even mine. From that moment on, I didn't know exactly what my mission was, but I did understand that I had to take care of ME 100 percent because I was truly valuable and important!

I realized that in order to have a different result in my life, I had to do something different to begin with. The answer came so easily — I knew I had to jump off my treadmill and do something so radical that it would make a major change in my life. For a fleeting moment I had the vision of some early explorer who burned his ships so that his soldiers couldn't rethink their decision to explore the New World and decide to return home!

I sensed that the overwhelming feeling of safety I had felt in Cozumel was given to me for a reason. I also knew all too well, that the gloom of the winter in the States only added to my chronic depression. It was a battle I fought every winter. Considering that it was early December, I could plan on a lot of snowy, cold, and dreary months ahead. The Cozumel sunshine called to me like the mother of any newborn creature. I knew in my heart that my recovery would occur fastest in this new paradise where I felt right at home.

So I went home, packed my bags, and told my friends I was going to move to Cozumel for six months of healing. Everyone immediately thought I was crazy. At first, I don't think they took me seriously. After all, it was going on Christmastime and everyone was getting wrapped up with their own holiday issues and since I looked calmer, they felt that I was back on solid ground and would simply get on with my life. I think they thought, "Yeah, everyone says they're going to move to paradise when they come home from someplace great. She'll get over it." But as I began to make plans for my decision to escape the American rat race and head somewhere beyond my usual, safe environment, they slowly started believing me.

I have to give my friends credit for not trying to stop me, although I did keep my eyes open, just in case someone decided that I truly was losing my mind and they should call the loony bin to take me away! (I actually wondered for a moment, if I could be committed by my concerned family for this "insane" maneuver!) Yet, I give them all my sincere thanks for having enough faith in me to know what was right for me at the time. I will always remember my mother especially, as she and another friend dropped me off at the airport. She cried as if she would never see me again. (I could just envision the nightmares she might have of guerilla soldiers dragging me off into some remote Mexican jungle, never to be seen again! How could she know that Cozumel is 100 percent tourist paradise since she'd never been there?) She showed huge strength at that moment, for which I will always be thankful.

Get Out of Your Boxx

What I learned on this journey was astounding! I had no car, no mail, no phone and no companion. I could be whoever I wanted to be, and as a 5'10" blonde with short, spiky hair, I definitely stood out in the crowd from the short, Mayan natives! I didn't speak Spanish and felt the awkwardness of being a foreigner in another's land. I spent many times in the midst of a group of people, all laughing and joking, and I hadn't a clue as to what they were talking about. Things as simple as getting my hair cut when I didn't speak the language was interesting, at best! I had to start asking people for help and learn to trust along the way.

I got a job at a hotel in a capacity similar to that of a concierge, and worked six days a week for peanuts. I rode the bus to and from work each day, standing out like a sore thumb as the only American amongst a sea of brown faces on short bodies. I cried a lot. I thought a lot. I slept a lot. I sat on the beach and talked to God a lot. But the best thing I did was to put life into perspective. Needless to say, it didn't happen overnight.

So many of my belief systems slowly came tumbling down, brick by brick, as I spent time living in a culture without the fast-paced, materialistic, "what everybody else thinks" philosophy Americans are surrounded by every day. I began to realize that my life didn't define me – rather, that *I* defined my life! It wasn't the job I held, the house I lived in, the vehicle I drove, the furniture I owned, or the friends I kept. My life was being true to myself and doing what was right for *me*. I had to learn to love and take care of myself first before I could love or care for anyone else. I also had to start understanding all the boxxes that had trapped me for so long and had sucked the very life out of me. They began to reveal themselves to me over time and I really started to slowly comprehend how they had affected me in three major areas of my life: my career, my relationships and my health.

The amazing part was that once I started unraveling the

idea about "Getting Out of the Boxx," I began to do a small research project of my own. Not real scientific research, mind you, just observational research. I started studying the Americans who came to Cozumel on vacation and I tried to guess which boxxes I thought they lived in! It was eye-opening and sad at the same time. So many people, unhappy or unfulfilled in their day-to-day life, seem to think that if they only go away on vacation, everything will be just fine! The truth is whatever their reality is in their "real" life, is the same reality no matter where they go. They just take it with them. I saw so many sad, unhappy, fearful, hateful, depressed people on vacation. Oh yes, many of them wear some great masks, but they can't hide what's inside. Many walk on eggshells around each other. I watched couples eat together and not ever speak. I saw fathers ignore their children on entire vacations. I witnessed single, lonely individuals begging to be loved. And I could just about tell you after a while, exactly which boxxes they lived in.

Besides my work on "boxx recognition," my healing continued in other ways. It took time to let my mind be "quiet enough" to hear my inner voice that had been "boxxed" up for so long; the voice that had been trying to tell me for years just what my true life passions were. I had always known that helping people had been a driving force for me. Certainly, that had contributed to my becoming a nurse to begin with. Yet this voice was demanding that I provide more than just physical care to people's bodies. I kept realizing that the life experiences I had gleaned could perhaps help others in some way. My love of teaching had always been a passion. Standing up in front of a live audience was always like a huge jolt of adrenaline for me. It didn't matter what the topic was – give me two thousand people and a topic I knew inside and out, and I was a happy camper. Although I had lectured for many organizations, even at some national conventions, I had never really found an ongoing outlet for this side of my nature.

I also rediscovered my passion for writing. Perhaps rediscovered isn't the right word, for I have written odds and ends of things for years. Maybe the more appropriate description is that I finally found something to write about that I was passionate about — the message being so strong that it drove me to stay up until all hours of the night, pouring the words out onto the paper. I had had enough foresight to purchase a used laptop computer to take with me to Cozumel. With it I journaled my daily adventures each night before bed, which were the original steps towards writing this book.

The message soon became clear to me. My mission from God was to teach others how to "live outside their boxxes," no matter what their labels, their history, their faith, or their personal stories. No, I don't expect them to "run away from home" like I did. Rather, I want to give them tools to help them see the powerful person within and all the possibilities that await each of us in life, if only we are open to them.

By living outside their self-limiting "boxxes" people can be true to themselves, and love themselves, so they can grow and give love in return. I want them to find the passion in their lives and not just the darkness, or the boredom, or the dull routine. I hope they can remember the excitement that used to drive them out of bed every morning when they were children — the excitement we all once had — in the great anticipation of what wonderful possibilities might be awaiting.

I wake up every morning now, thanking God for each and every wonderful day. I also believe even more strongly in the statement that God gives you only as much as he knows you can handle and no more. I know now that He had a plan for me for a long time – I just had to find it.

My hope for you is that reading this might light a small spark in you to find your true direction in the journey you are on by learning to get out of your boxxes, whatever they might be. You might be dealing with some big issues, or you may have lived a charmed life and all is working well, but your mission might be to always find a way to make each day even more wonderful and fulfilling. Regardless, I invite you to study and examine your boxxes, and decide which path is calling you. Once you know how to break down the walls of your roadblocks, you will discover your best life ever and the many, many possibilities that await you along the way!

Happy traveling and God bless!

"I was dirt-poor, blind, you name it. Yet, here I am today."

Ray Charles

Chapter 2
Rediscovering
The World Of Possibilities

First of all, let me explain that I am not a trained therapist, minister, or a life coach. I have no research statistics that prove anything you are about to read. I am just one person who has gone on a journey of personal growth in a rather non-traditional manner. That journey changed my life. The thoughts I am sharing with you are my own personal beliefs about life and some of the challenges that life often hands us. This belief system may speak to you, or it may not. Either way is OK. My hope for you is that you find *something* that works for you. We are so fortunate to live in a time when there are hundreds of powerful messages surrounding us as we seek our own direction on our journeys through life. My wish for you is that you find one that fits your heart and mind and spirit.

"Getting Out of the Boxx" is all about recognizing the many possibilities that await you in life. It is a way of looking at things differently. Of taking your blinders off. Of opening your mind to examining not only yourself, but your past, your responses to your world, and your attitudes, and then deciding which direction you want to go. It is about making choices and realizing that even by making a decision *not* to decide, you *are* deciding.

To begin the process, use your imagination and your memory and pretend with me for just a minute. I want you to think back to when you were five years old and it was Christ-

Rediscovering The World of Possibilities

mas Eve. Your parents had just tucked you in bed and told you that Santa Claus would come during the night and awaiting you in the morning would be wonderful presents and exciting things beyond your wildest dreams! As they left you in your room, you wondered how on Earth they could possibly believe you could go to sleep with that much excitement hanging heavily upon you! The world of "possibilities" that awaited you in the morning was absolutely overwhelming to your young mind!

You took forever to fall asleep, tossing and turning, the adrenaline in your system suggesting sleep was unnecessary at best. You awoke several times, but realizing it was still nighttime and Santa Claus only came if no one was looking, you stayed in your room, lest you surprise him and he leave without finishing his job! At last, when you couldn't stand it one minute longer, you jumped out of bed, flew down the stairs, and raced to see what was under the Christmas tree! The anticipation of all those wonderful "possibilities" couldn't hold you one minute longer, because you knew there could be something so wonderful there it could change your life!

Do you remember those feelings? Your heart beating fast from excitement! Your brain going a thousand miles an hour! Your body tuned up and ready to pounce! Can you also remember wondering why on Earth you were the only one up that early?

The reason for all the behaviors you exhibited at that time in your life had to do with the anticipation of something exciting about to happen which would make that day extraordinary! It gave you energy, a spring in your step, a spark in your eye, a smile on your face. It made your heart sing and your muscles spring into action. It made you healthy and happy and well adjusted. You were on top of the world and probably felt like you could accomplish anything!

OK, now fast forward to today. First of all, how did you sleep last night? Did you toss and turn with excitement and anticipation like you did that Christmas Eve, or were you restless because you were worried about what might happen at work today? Were you having nightmares about not getting a promotion at work, or fussing about the guy in the next cubicle who drives you crazy? Maybe you were concerned that your husband won't be happy with the idea that you'd really like to go back to school but the only way you can afford it is if he takes care of the kids three evenings a week and you don't know how he'll take to the idea. Or might you be dreaming of getting a different job because the one you have leaves you feeling empty and bored to tears, but it pays well and there aren't a lot of other jobs to choose from, so maybe you should just be thankful you have it?

My next question to you is this: How many times did you hit the snooze alarm this morning? Once, twice, three times? More? Why? What is it about life that leaves you wishing you could stay in bed all day instead of flying out of bed like that five year old you once were on Christmas Day? Have you quit seeing the possibilities that surround you each and every day? Possibilities that can still make every day full of surprises and might change your life?

What happened to all those possibilities?

I realize that your life is fast, hectic, frenzied, exciting, fun, filled with people and places and responsibilities and bills and tasks and chores and so on and so on and so on. Yet, admit it, does it seem more often than not, like you're a hamster on a treadmill? The "treadmill of life?" Each Sunday do you look ahead to the week and just can't wait for the next weekend because the five days in between not only don't fill you with a sense of excitement, they fill you with a sense of boredom, or possibly even dread?

Or maybe you're one of the lucky ones who has already mastered a variety of things and you feel on top of the world,

Rediscovering The World of Possibilities

but what worries you is each time you accomplish something new and wonderful you wonder if there will be anything else to replace it. What if you run out of new and exciting things to do with your life?

Either way, the possibilities are always around us, but it seems as we grow up we tend to lose sight of them. That's where the "boxxes" come in. We start letting ourselves get boxxed in by so many things we start to lose sight of the fact that exciting possibilities still surround us each and every day, if only we are open to seeing them.

Look at children again for a moment. If you asked a group of kindergarteners if they can scuba dive, do you know what they would say? Well, most of the group would frantically wave their hands in the air and say, "I can, I can!" Why? *Because they don't yet know they can't!* They are open to all the possibilities life throws at them because they haven't yet developed boxxes. They are ready to tackle the world! They probably don't even know what scuba diving is, but that doesn't hold them back.

Would you like that energy again? That excitement? That open-mindedness? That pure love of life that you had when you were that age? Well, it's there for those who believe they can have it. Look around you and I'll bet you know at least one person like that in your life. Probably not dozens, but at least one. That's the person who always has so much energy that you wonder what they're taking and you'd like to know where they buy it! They are always happy, upbeat, positive, rarely seem to let anything get them upset, are always friendly and helpful to others wherever they go. The eternal optimist, even when times get rough. They always find the silver lining in each and every gray cloud.

If you can't think of anyone immediately, there are so many famous people whose stories you might relate to. Nelson Mandela, imprisoned for years for his political beliefs, had every right to evolve through that ordeal into an angry, vengeful, hateful man, and yet, quite the opposite is true. Martin Luther King maintained a belief system of kindness and love in the face of hatred and pain. Helen Keller surmounted overwhelming limitations to take her place in history as a true survivor and an example of overwhelming success.

While all these examples may seem extreme to you, there are everyday people who prevail as well. For example, a young Colorado man severed his own arm to save his life after being pinned by an enormous boulder while hiking. The eternal optimist, he found a way to live and thanked God and his family for praying for him around the clock until he persevered through the darkness to find the light. Before leaving the hospital on his road to physical recovery, he was already making plans for his next outdoor adventure.

If these people can overcome such odds of enormous proportion, then doesn't it seem possible that most of us should be able to find a way to enjoy our lives more fully? Finding joy in the simple things should be easy. Awaking each day looking forward to the wondrous possibilities that surround us should be as common as breathing.

Whether you are a man or a woman, (and I will use examples of each throughout this book), if you begin by believing that your life is all about choices, then you are ready to begin to examine your boxxes and to decide whether they are helping you or holding you back. All the possibilities are there. Just knowing that can be empowering. It's all up to you.

"Most people see what is and never see what can be."
Albert Einstein

Chapter 3
What Boxx ?

The expression "thinking out of the box" has been around for quite some time. As a matter of fact, if you do a *Google* search for the phrase, using the traditional spelling, there are over 350,000 pages of information! (Out of the Boxx with two x's still has 360 pages!) Oprah Winfrey has even done a show on the concept. Yet, has anyone ever stopped to ask themselves exactly what "the box" is?

Actually, I believe there are many boxxes: Fear, Your Past, Perfectionism, Workaholism, Emptiness, The Victim, Depression, Denial, and many, many more. I'm sure some of you even have your own specific, personal boxxes. But no matter what they are, they overlap into three major areas of your life: Your career, your relationships, and your health.

The important thing is to identify the boxxes affecting your life and decide if they are working for or against you. I believe all of our boxxes start out as good things. In fact, some of them are important to keep.

Let me give you an example. One of the boxxes you'll learn about in Chapter 4 is Fear. If we didn't have fear in life, we would likely risk injury or death on a daily basis. If I had no fear at all, I could try jumping off of a twenty-story building, which would not be wise. Instead, as very young children we begin to learn protective behaviors to keep us from falling prey to situations that might hurt us.

Visualize yourself wearing a small, fitted boxx, the size

Get Out of Your Boxx

of a bullet-proof vest. It protects your vital organs, yet allows flexibility of movement of your arms and legs and is small enough that it still lets you pass through doors while wearing it. I like to think back to the first New World explorers. Their body armor only protected their trunk, unlike the heavy, cumbersome full suits of armor worn by "knights in shining armor." It was relatively lightweight but protective enough to save their lives; at the same time, it allowed them to see in all directions, unlike the earlier, full-body versions.

Boxxes like this are helpful. The healthy, Body Armor sized Boxx of Fear I described earlier can be lifesaving without imposing limitations or blocking your view of the great possibilities of life.

When I visualize Living Out of the Boxx, I like to picture myself in a room. As I stand in the middle of the room, I am surrounded by open doors on all sides of me — in front, behind, and on both sides. These doors represent life's possibilities. They are wide open, allowing things to come to me, or me to walk through to discover them.

If I am wearing that small boxx, I have full view of all the doors at any given time.

However, if my boxx becomes larger and larger, it can eventually engulf me and then my view is completely obstructed! And voilà — I'm "stuck" in my boxx in a room whose doors I have also become too big to pass through!

So, how do our boxxes get so big? Well, that depends upon the boxx itself. If we are talking about Fear, think about how a baby learns to walk. There is a certain amount of fear taking place during this development. Although their thoughts are very simple, they recognize that each time they attempt to

Get Out of Your Boxx

take those first, scary steps, they fall down a lot! Sometimes there's a bruised knee or chin or other painful reminder of the experience. Perhaps each of these painful moments gives the child cause for pause, and walking is put on hold for a while. Although fear is a much simpler picture for their immature minds, it is nonetheless present.

If we stop and remember that all of us learned to walk at some point, it becomes apparent that the child's tiny Boxx of Fear was overcome by the desire to walk and catch up with the rest of the kids! The fear of that first step was less important than being left behind by the others!

Now let's expand this concept to an adult who lives in a Boxx of Fear. Does someone who is lonely and seeking romance, refuse to date again because they have had some bad dating experiences? If so, then the Boxx of Fear has grown from body armor size to that of a small house! It locks the person within its four walls where they *think* they are safe. After all, no one can hurt them if they don't let them in, right? While this might be true, what has happened to their ability to see life's possibilities? What if Mr. Right walked in the door, but the tightly boxxed person doesn't even see him? What wonderful things might they be missing? This is how hiding in your boxx can be detrimental rather than protective.

So How Do You Get Out of Your Boxx?

First, ask yourself lots of questions to help identify your own boxxes. Unfortunately, it's not a quick, cut-and-dried process. It's not like taking your measurements or weighing yourself and knowing exactly where you stand! It will take some introspection, some examination of your past, and even asking your closest friends and/or family members for help with this analysis. (Be sure to only ask those people whose opinion you can trust. If your spouse has been critical of you in the past, he or she is not going to be your best ally now!)

What Boxx?

Read the following list of questions and see if any of them ring a bell. They are broad, general statements that may give you a clue as to whether you are possibly "stuck in a boxx." They may also give you a desire to probe deeper. If you feel a twinge of fear or apprehension about answering any of them, or if you don't have an immediate answer, it's a good sign that it may be a good starting place for you. Then, as you read each chapter about the individual boxxes, see if any of the descriptions sound familiar and start your search from there. Be honest, open, and willing to accept change into your life! If you are, the results can be incredible!

Do You:
- ❏ Feel like your life is stuck in a rut? Like a hamster on the wheel doing the same thing day after day, with no change in sight?
- ❏ Feel your professional life is great, but your personal relationships are lacking or non-existent? (Or vice versa.) You feel competent, respected and valued in one of those areas, but not in the other.
- ❏ Feel that you live your life for your family and get your needs met last, if ever?
- ❏ Wake up every morning dreading getting out of bed because there's nothing to look forward to? How many times do you shut off the alarm before you finally get up?
- ❏ Fight chronic fatigue or depression, and don't know why?
- ❏ Hate the dull, boring routine in your life, but don't know how to change it?
- ❏ Wish for things you believe to be impossible — winning the lottery to solve your financial problems, losing a lot of weight, finding a loving relationship, getting a better job? Or even just having more time to spend with your family?

Get Out of Your Boxx

- ❏ Feel lost trying to decide what to do with your life? Perhaps you raised your children or sold your business or retired, and now you just don't know what to do with your time?
- ❏ Become easily frustrated about things?
- ❏ When you do have free time do you know what you might want to do to fill it?
- ❏ Do you even allow yourself free time?

Use these examples to begin asking yourself where you are now and where you want to go.

Let me give you an example that might help you see a bigger picture of someone and her boxxes.

Rachel

Rachel is a nurse, mother, and wife. That is how she defines herself first and foremost. Within this self-definition, she is also chef, housekeeper, and chauffeur for her two children. Her husband works too, so she feels that these are *her* roles at home. She "wishes" she could go back to school to get her master's degree, but believes she is too old and doesn't know when she would find the time Yet, by getting additional education she would have more job opportunities that may prove more fun and interesting. At the same time it would increase her income potential. She is unhappy with her weight, but she's convinced that her family genes are the cause since her siblings and parents are all overweight as well. She believes she will never be able to lose weight, no matter how hard she tries. She knows that her cholesterol is high and she would like to do something about that too, but since she's only 40 and doesn't have high blood pressure, she's not extremely worried about her risk of heart disease yet. She comes home from work tired and stressed, and drops in a heap on the couch for her only thirty minutes of peace before picking up the kids from school. She feels as if her life is in a rut, but sees no way out. She wishes she had more one-on-one time with her husband, but with their crazy schedules there are few opportunities. She looks ahead to a time when her children are grown and when life might be able to slow down a bit and let her enjoy it more.

Can you see the many boxxes Rachel has built for herself? She feels she has no time to do anything for herself, and yet, she has boxxed herself into the role of the only chef, housekeeper, and chauffeur. We don't know her husband's career, but if she is like many women, she simply takes on those chores because she is the "woman of the house." Has she ever asked her husband or children to help with these tasks or would she feel guilty doing so? (The Boxx of Guilt seems to come naturally to many women!) She says that she would like to go back to school, but wouldn't be able to find the time, yet has she examined how to free up some time by reorganizing her family, arranging after school daycare, or hiring someone to clean her house?

Her weight and cholesterol are big issues but she is not taking them seriously and rationalizes that obesity runs in her family. Thus, she is stuck with this fate. If she continues to believe this way, it won't matter what diet she tries, for she has already convinced herself that she will fail.

She keeps looking ahead to when her children are grown, convinced that life will finally "slow down," at last allowing her to spend time with her husband and do some things for herself. Too bad she believes those times are so far away.

With all of these overlapping issues, Rachel is only perpetuating what she has built for herself – a confining boxx that allows no room for change, self expression, or personal growth. Yet at the root of her issues, perhaps Rachel's underlying message to herself is that she just isn't important enough to change. She may not yet have come to believe that she

Get Out of Your Boxx

needs to *take care of herself first* before she can effectively take care of those she loves.

Rachel is not uncommon. There are hundreds of thousands of Rachels. They are not abnormal or maladjusted. It's not to say their lives are not filled with fun, excitement, or rewards. They experience love, the joy of raising their families, success at their careers, and other wonderful times. Yet, how much *better* might they be if they got "Out Of Their Boxxes" and opened themselves to the many possibilities awaiting them? Even if everything in their lives were functioning at a 10, wouldn't it be great to be a 12 or 15?

All is possible when you know how to "Get Out of Your Boxx!"

"When a man knows what he wants, he will move heaven and Earth to get it."
                                                    Unknown

Part Two
Identifying Your Boxxes

*L*et's begin to identify and examine various boxxes, some of which you might recognize. This is only a partial list of the many, many boxxes we can all get stuck in. You may not find your own here, and that's quite alright! Just study yours in the same way you study these, and ask that ever important question: Is it working for you or holding you back?

"If you do nothing, nothing happens."
                                    Evelyn Kaye

Chapter 4
Fear: The Biggest Boxx Of All

As I sat at my computer the night I wrote my suicide letter, the Boxx of Fear had me in a death grip – literally. Although at the time, I could not have told you it was fear that I was dealing with. Yet, if you would have been there to observe my behaviors and emotions, what you would have seen was overwhelming sadness, gut-wrenching pain, depths of depression, furious anger, and a strong desire to be heard. I sobbed to the point of almost being unable to breathe. The tears streamed down my face like a torrential rainstorm. My muscles were so taut they ached, my stomach knotted to the point of pain, and my faced flushed with obvious elevation in blood pressure. Although the label of fear was not showing, the physical symptoms were, whether I recognized them or not.

Fortunately, that survival Boxx of Body Armor I mentioned earlier — the boxx that can be a good thing – saved my life. I was more afraid of hurting the ones I loved than of the more generalized fears that drove me to that point of desperation. Yet what were my exact fears?

To sum it up as best as I can, now that time and perspective have given me greater understanding, I would say that the most overwhelming fear I carried was one of not feeling valuable to anyone, including myself. Others were the fear of being unloved, of being alone, and of the unknown.

Do you live in the Boxx known as Fear? It is the

Fear: The Biggest Boxx of All

"Mother of them all," so to speak, for the other boxxes all branch off in one way or another from this one. The Boxx of Fear is multidimensional: Fear of failure, of success, of loss, of losing love or attention, of loneliness, of physical or emotional pain, of ridicule, or of being wrong. There are many more, but these represent the tip of the iceberg. Behaviors and feelings such as anger, frustration, depression, sadness, humor, and even sarcasm may all reflect some kind of fear. Fears can be specific or general, known or unknown, justifiable or totally in our imagination.

The Boxx of Fear locks you in by limiting the choices, opportunities, and possibilities you can discover and enjoy in life.

Fear of failure, for example, may keep you from trying a new business venture that might have otherwise provided you with a sense of accomplishment and excitement, and maybe even more financial security in the long run.

Fear of physical or emotional pain might keep you in a bad relationship because you may worry that your partner will inflict more abuse on you if you threaten to leave. Yet by not leaving, you may risk abuse to other family members as well.

Fear of being wrong might keep you silent in a brainstorming meeting at work where you have the perfect solution for a problem but are afraid of being laughed at by coworkers who might not agree with you. Not speaking up and bringing that great idea to the surface might mean the promotion you want goes to someone else!

Allowing your teenager to run over the top of you might be your way of dealing with your fear that they might not love you if you put boundaries on them. However, research has shown that most teenagers are begging for boundaries and are usually pushing you to find just where those boundaries are.

Perhaps you are in an unsatisfying relationship but the fear of being alone outweighs your frustration about not feeling loved. Yet, the point you miss is that as long as you're involved with "Mr. Wrong," it's unlikely that "Mr. Right" will ever find you.

Do you stay inside the Boxx of Fear because it is a known entity, and the big "unknown" outside looks even scarier? Would you like to break out of the stifling space you're living in?

Then the most important question to ask yourself is this: What would you do differently if you weren't afraid? How might you feel if you knew that your new business couldn't possibly fail? What if you could be free from your unsatisfying relationship and could be with someone who treated you with respect? Someone you could spend the rest of your life with feeling happy, safe, and unconditionally loved?

These are not impossible dreams – but they are *guaranteed* unattainable if you stay trapped within your Boxx of Fear. Begin by realizing that wonderful possibilities are truly attainable and are within your reach. Then ask yourself which fears are holding you back. You can't slay your dragon unless you know what he or she looks like.

After returning from Mexico and beginning my new business venture, I got stuck in some fearful boxxes for a while. I kept worrying, "What if it fails? What if I spend all this money for nothing?" The day I wrote my first big business check for brochures and artwork, my heart was in my throat! Then it occurred to me that while people all over this country have been chasing the stock market up and down with their money, I was investing in *myself*. Only I knew just how hard I was willing to work towards my dream, and if I couldn't rely on myself to get the job done, why would I rely on anyone else to determine the direction of my life for me? This recognition helped me to start breaking down the walls of my Boxx of Fear of Failure.

Someone once told me that there are really only two emotions — fear and love — and that most of us spend our

Fear: The Biggest Boxx of All

lives either trying to run away from fear, or towards love. I think that rather equates to the "glass half full or half empty" analogy of life views of the pessimist versus the optimist.

With this assumption in mind, I have listed various behaviors or words I thought might fit into each category. This list could go on and on, but I think you get the trend…

FEAR	**LOVE**
Anger	Happiness
Sadness	Caring
Frustration	Kindness
Anxiety	Comfort
Depression	Giving
Hostility	Understanding
Withdrawal	Listening
Silence	Compassion
Resentment	Empathy
Hurt	Unconditionality
Sarcastic humor	Sacrifice

If fear is the overriding boxx from which the others evolve, then love is the opposing direction so many of us are hoping for. Yet, I think they are incredibly intertwined in more ways than that.

In my journey of self-discovery, the most profound realization I had was that if I didn't take care of myself and love ME first, then how could I ever truly love or take care of anyone else? This could be as simple as taking physical care of myself so I lived as long as possible to be here for my loved ones, or as complex as loving myself deeply enough to accept myself as I am, thus being better able to accept my loved ones as they are — without judgment, qualifiers, or conditions. Another simple example of this is obvious during the pre-flight directions the flight attendants always give passengers on every airline: "In case of emergency, adjust your OWN oxygen first, and then assist your child with his." They realize first-hand that if the adult passes out from lack of oxygen, she surely isn't going to be able to help her child.

Yet, you may have to battle a lot of fears to love yourself first. Fear that people will think you are conceited or selfish, for starters. We have all been taught there is a fine line between loving yourself and loving yourself too much! There certainly is an array of superstars whose apparent self-love goes way beyond the norm. Yet, do these people truly love themselves, or do they overcompensate for their insecurities by developing behaviors they think will make them strong and proud? Are they hiding their fears behind a big mask of grandiosity so that no one will recognize their real issues? (You will learn about the boxx called Narcissism in a later chapter.)

People who truly love themselves are comfortable with who they are. They do not need the approval of others to validate their existence or behaviors. They give unconditionally. They accept people for who they are. They do not fear rejection. They recognize that life is about choices and that they cannot control the behaviors of others. They can only control their responses to others and their own attitudes, beliefs, and feelings. They have found an inner peace. For when it comes to the relationship they have with themselves, they have mastered that aspect of the Boxx of Fear.

Had I loved myself more at that very dark time in my life, the thought of suicide would have never crossed my mind. I would have never even allowed myself to fall into the well of depression to begin with. I would have realized that I am a valuable person who brings something important to the table of life. I cannot control anyone but me, and I have complete and total control over how I react to absolutely everyone in my life. The feelings of sadness, anger, and hopelessness would never have gotten a chance to get their hooks in me to begin with, had I learned to love ME and care for ME, first and foremost.

Fear: The Biggest Boxx of All

Boxxes And Boxxes And Boxxes Of Fears

Fear is learned from the time we are infants and grows with us throughout life. While specific fears may be hard for you to identify or to label, the words listed earlier under the column of Fear, may help lead you to your own discovery. For example, maybe you've been feeling "frustrated" lately. Frustrated by what? Let's say you're frustrated with your job. Now start being specific. Ask yourself exactly what frustrates you. Perhaps you're frustrated because you got passed over for a promotion again. Now dig a little deeper. Ask yourself why you were passed over. Was it truly your qualifications, or do you think that the boss liked someone else better? If that is what you believe, ask yourself the next question: At what other time in your life did you feel you were rejected because someone in a powerful position liked someone else more than you? Perhaps your big brother always took your other sibling with him on outings and wouldn't take you, and all you really wanted was for your big brother to love you. So is the fear you are really feeling underneath your frustration, fear of rejection perhaps?

Or are you feeling angry about something? Perhaps you are angry at your boyfriend who promised to call you and didn't – again! Get more specific – why are you feeling angry? What thoughts go through your mind? Are you angry because you feel ignored? Do you feel his behavior demonstrates that he doesn't really love you, despite his words to the contrary? Do you feel that you must not be important enough in his life because he doesn't take the time to show you his love, and that by this omission, he is really telling you the truth through his actions and not his words? If any of these are true, how can they be tied to fear? Well, feeling ignored and not valued could strike a core fear of not feeling important in life. It could raise the fear of rejection. The fear of ending up alone. Combine all of those underneath your fear "umbrella," and the real

Get Out of Your Boxx

issue is that you are afraid of being rejected and alone, and not important enough to anybody in the world!

Now, obviously, that's a pretty big leap, but you get the idea. If you dig deeply enough, you start to get to the real fears. Once you can break out of the boxxes that confine you, your entire attitude and behavior style can change.

Using this same example, consider this. What if you had no fear of rejection, being alone, and having no value? Instead, what if you loved yourself enough to believe that you are valued, you are a wonderful person, and that wonderful people attract wonderful people into their lives? What possibilities might open up to you? If you were without a boyfriend you wouldn't think of it as the end of the world. You might see it as the time for self-growth while you wait for the right person to come into your life! See the difference?

The next important thing about your fears is realizing that once you face them, you begin to have power over them. Not only do you realize you can handle things that you may not have thought possible, this reality has the ability to overlap into other areas of your life. My giant leap Out of the Boxx going to Mexico helped me to see that I was certainly capable of taking on new activities – many of which I would have normally considered to be outside my ability and/or my comfort zone. I remember riding mopeds years ago in Belize. I was scared to death the whole time as I had to drive by myself. Well, I not only mastered riding one in Cozumel, I bought a used one and became quite adept at maneuvering around the island. I have even weighed the possibility of trying out real motorcycles at some point in my future! If you had asked me two years ago if I would ever own a moped, I would have said you were crazy! Yet, opening one door led to building self-confidence in other areas of my life as well. It was like a domino effect!

Fear can be paralyzing, whether the issue you're facing is small or large. I remember a woman named Jill in my scuba

Fear: The Biggest Boxx of All

diving class years ago. We were learning our skills in the pool and had spent the first day practicing all the basics. Upon returning to the class the second day, we all suited up and were supposed to take our "giant stride" entry into the pool. This meant taking a big step off of the edge of the pool into the eight foot deep water, while wearing all the equipment. Since we had spent several hours the preceding day performing these very basic skills, everyone quickly donned the gear and jumped into the pool. Everyone, that is, except Jill. While the rest of us were following our instructor underwater, in anticipation of the new lessons for the day, she was frozen in fear standing at the edge of the pool. She had her equipment on, had one foot lifted in a position ready to jump, but had suddenly become totally and completely paralyzed by fear.

Logically, there should have been no reason for her panic. She had performed beautifully the preceding day and was very comfortable in the water. She had been excited to get certified as she and her husband were heading on a diving vacation within days, and yet she remained paralyzed by some overwhelming fear that none of the rest of us could see. Exactly what she was afraid of, I never knew. Fortunately, we had wonderful instructors and while one of them took the rest of us on to our next lesson, the second stayed in the water and simply talked to Jill for about twenty minutes until she felt comfortable taking that very important first step. His calm, caring attitude helped her get "Out of her Boxx" and she became a certified diver.

My point is, if something relatively small can paralyze someone, what effect might something really big have upon your life? What if you lost your job and were a single mother with three kids to feed? It becomes easy to see how easily overwhelming things can become.

The Boxxes of Fear are very powerful forces in our lives, but they *are* surmountable. The first step is discovery. Unfortunately, fear can be convoluted, confusing, and complex. With that in mind, I have outlined my system of "boxxes" to help you better pinpoint your specific fear through the behaviors defined within the boxxes themselves. While it may be difficult to realize that your fear is really fear of failure, it might be much easier to identify your Boxx of Perfectionism. Then, learning what drives the perfectionist, you may begin to understand what your true Fear Boxxes really are.

Keep in mind that we all are bound to have some fears in our lives, and we are all "works in progress." We are ever changing. What I was frightened of as a teenager may be dramatically different than what frightens me at age 47. Reading this book today may yield some answers based upon what stress and situations are going on in your life right now. Then, reading it again five years from now may help you find more clues to the complex individual you are, as different life issues confront you. While the underlying fears may still be the same, your approach to them, combined with the situations you face in life at that time, may reveal new information to you in your quest on the road to discoveries about you!

In addition, common sense needs to prevail. Just because your heart's desire is to start your own business, it doesn't mean that you shouldn't have that healthy, helpful Body Armor Boxx to keep you in balance. You don't want to throw good money after bad if the business is obviously a mistake.

A friend of mine used to constantly wish his family could be reunited again after a divorce. Although he and his ex-wife are like oil and water when they are together, the image in his mind was of family unity. One day he told me he believed what Anthony Robbins, the renowned motivator said, "Whatever you *really* want in life is attainable, if you just put your mind to it." I smiled and agreed, but I told him that what he hadn't heard Mr. Robbins say was that common sense still has to prevail. I related my heart's desire to him — I want to eat five pounds of chocolate every day. I really, really want it. And there's nothing to stop me from getting it. However, five pounds of chocolate every day is NOT healthy for anybody! I need to use some common sense! In his case, he may have tried a thousand ways to reunite his family, and perhaps with his sheer will and determination, he might have accomplished the task. Yet, I asked him, "Is it healthy for any of you?" When he looked at it that way, he recognized that his reality and his dream were two different things, and that he had lost his ability to see the big picture in the process. There's a fine line between facing your fears and pursuing your dreams versus taking on risks that are truly unrealistic.

There are probably hundreds of books written about fear. Each has its own unique style or philosophy. You may wish to study this subject in much greater detail to better understand the deeper issues that hold you in your particular Boxx of Fear.

As you face your fears and break out of the boxxes holding you back, your life may take many different avenues. Opportunities you may have missed may become visible to you once again.

Now that you know that fear is the "mother boxx," let's see how understanding the sub-boxxes might help you on your path of self-discovery!

Get Out of Your Boxx

"Do one thing that scares you every day... after a while there won't be many things left that scare you!"

Unknown

Chapter 5
"I Can't, I Should, I Have To !"

During my stay in Mexico I had a job similar to that of a hotel concierge. The best part was that I arranged a great deal with the dive shop – I sent them new customers and rather than pay me a commission, they let me scuba dive for free. I was thrilled! My prior diving experiences had been limited to the typical week-long vacation we took every couple of years, which meant that I dove perhaps six or eight times every year, if I was lucky. Not the best way to become good at it. This opportunity let me practice, practice, practice! I usually finished work just in time to catch the last boat of the day which was the one that always took the new student divers. This was fine with me because diving with them only helped build my confidence since I was always better than they were! Then one day as Luis the dive instructor was telling the students what the plan was, he pointed out that while he would be at the front of the group leading the way, I would be at the back of the group in case the students at the back needed any help. I was stunned! He made it sound like I knew what the heck I was doing! My confidence soared!

My comfort level began to increase by leaps and bounds as I racked up the dives and religiously recorded them in my log book! I really started to feel like a pro. Then one day Luis told me he was teaching an Advanced Diver Certification Course, and his students were doing a night dive. Wouldn't I like to go along?

Get Out of Your Boxx

My heart began to pound frantically, my palms started to sweat, and I felt my throat start to tighten. I barely croaked out the words, "I-I-I can't." Not understanding my reaction, he stopped and looked at me rather oddly for a minute, and then he asked why I couldn't go. As my heart continued to race, I sheepishly admitted, "I can't possibly do that — I'm claustrophobic!"

He looked at me quizzically and said, "So? You dive during the day. What's the difference?" I felt as though my new-found confidence had just had the rug pulled right out from under it!

To me, the difference was even more profound than night and day – it was terrifying! My Boxx of Claustrophobia was truly overpowering. (A boxx I'll talk about further in another chapter.) The thought of not easily seeing my way out of that environment clutched at my entire soul. My Boxx of Fear of the Unknown engulfed me like a hurricane. What if I hated it and wanted to go to the surface? Doing so would ruin someone else's dive since safe diving rules dictate that divers pair up and always stay with their buddy! If one must surface, so must the other, and all the others would be paying people. What would I do? I just HAD to say no!

The funny thing is that I had actually been on a night dive some years before; however, the circumstances had been quite different. We had taken our open water certification class at a hotel with a pier and drop-off that immediately fell to 25 feet of water. We dove this spot a half dozen times during our testing, so it was kind of like our back yard. The hotel was right there and we could step onto dry land at any time. So, the day we became certified we decided to dive at night, in our own comfortable "playground." It was very exciting, but six years had elapsed and the good memories had faded. The thought of jumping off a boat into black water in the middle of the ocean sent shock waves down my spine, and my I Can't Boxx simply took over automatically.

I Can't, I Should, I Have To!

Other diver friends had previously invited me to dive with them at night, and I had always brushed it off, telling them versions of the "I can't" story, but making light of it at the same time: "I can't because I have to work," or "I can't because I'm going out tonight," or any number of other stories. They were all just excuses. The bigger Boxx of Fear had me by the throat and I didn't even know why. I certainly didn't believe that sharks came out to feed on unsuspecting tourist divers every night or the dive business would have folded years ago!

The problem was that Luis just stood there staring at me, waiting for the answer to his question. If I wasn't claustrophobic diving during the day, why did I think I would be at night? I couldn't answer him and he wouldn't let me weasel out of it! At last I agreed, but with the stipulation that he understood I would be so close to him that it would be as though I was in his wetsuit with him! I wasn't kidding!

I also made him promise me that we would make our descent before the sky was absolutely pitch dark, so I could make the transition to darkness a little easier. He accepted my conditions and I tried to get my mind prepared for the dive. However, he didn't tell me one very important thing until the group briefing on the boat just before we got into the water. That one thing would make my heart start pounding again! He told us that there would be a few moments when he would signal us to sit on the ocean floor together and we would all turn off our flashlights at the same time for a few minutes. This was to observe an underwater phenomenon known as "bioluminescence." (Yes, you dive at night with flashlights and had I known about turning off the flashlights before I had committed to this adventure, there would have been NO WAY that I would have gone! Of course, Luis probably knew that too.)

So, there I was, stuck.

Get Out of Your Boxx

I went.

Hyperventilating during much of the descent, I kept telling myself no harm would come to me as I was with a trained instructor, who was also a friend, and he would certainly not let anything bad happen to me. I also prayed a lot! As the dive progressed I began to see the incredible beauty of the reef at night. I saw sea creatures that only come out with the darkness. My fears began to diminish and were replaced by excitement! During the daytime a multitude of bright, colorful fish are seemingly everywhere in Cozumel. But those same fish at night are hidden in small crevices and cracks in the reef and when discovered with a flashlight, stare back at you like a child hoping not to be found during a game of hide and seek! However, lobsters, octopus, and huge king crabs all journey out of their daytime retreats to hunt at night. They were magnificent! (I have a really hard time looking at live lobsters in the seafood department of my grocery store now, as I want to set them all free!)

Just as my fears were dissolving, Luis signaled for us to sit on the sand and indicated that we should turn off our flashlights. My stomach started jumping with anxiety again. I gulped hard and turned mine off with the others. It wasn't exactly pitch dark, but it was dark enough. The next thing he did was too beautiful to behold. He simply waved his arm through the water, and a small fireworks display suddenly appeared, dancing and glittering before our eyes! It was the phenomenon he had told us about. I am not a scientist, so I will put it in layman's terms. It has something to do with a chemical excreted by the reef. When the water is stirred up in a dark environment it creates the most beautiful shimmering light show that you can imagine. It was almost as though a small army of fireflies had suddenly stormed past us in the blink of an eye! What an experience! My heart started pumping with excitement, not anxiety!

I Can't, I Should, I Have To!

The entire adventure was exhilarating, powerful, phenomenal, and an opportunity I am glad I didn't miss! The best part was a week later when I returned to night diving with an entirely different group of people, including a dive master I didn't really know personally. I had a friend visiting from the States and enjoyed sharing the experience with her. In addition, my confidence about the entire dive experience had grown by leaps and bounds in just that short time, and I realized by then it had begun to trickle over into other parts of my island experience as well.

So what is the point of all of this?

What if I had stuck to my original response of, "I can't"? What if I had missed those incredible experiences? Not only did I see creatures I had never seen before, but the increased self-esteem created that night only added to my arsenal of weaponry against my Boxx of Fear.

How many times do you automatically say, "I can't," without even considering an opportunity presented to you? How many times do you talk yourself out of doing something you really want to do, but just don't think you can master? The Boxx of "I Can't" is sinister, devastating, and VERY easy to fall into.

Here are some "I can't" statements. See if any of them ring a bell for you…

- ❑ I can't go back to school – I'm too old.
- ❑ I can't learn to ski – I just can't risk getting hurt with three little kids to take care of.
- ❑ I can't afford it.
- ❑ I can't lose weight.
- ❑ I can't stop smoking.
- ❑ I can't ask for a promotion. My boss might get angry with me.
- ❑ I can't change jobs now. I've got such great benefits and vacation with this one. How could I ever find

one to match this?
- ❏ I can't go out with you on Friday night because I'd have to ask my husband to stay home with the kids.
- ❏ I can't go on vacation without my family. It just wouldn't be right.
- ❏ I can't tell my girlfriend how I really feel about that. She might not love me anymore.
- ❏ I can't go – I just don't have time.

I could write pages and pages of "I can't" statements here, but you get the idea.

What things are you saying "I can't" to in life? More importantly, why? What possibilities might open up if you said, "I can"? Henry Ford said, "Whether you think you can, or you think you can't – you're right!" The subconscious brain is more than happy to believe and deliver any messages that our conscious brain offers up, and constantly telling yourself "I can't" about so many things in your life simply reinforces to you that you are exactly right – no matter what – you JUST CAN'T. Whatever your "I can't" situation is, you have the power to change it, but you must make the conscious choice to do so.

Other treacherous phrases that can easily boxx you in are "I should," and "I have to." Now put all three of those together and you have one confining boxx!

Try this example on for size:

"I'm sorry Tommy, *I can't* go watch you play ball this Saturday because *I have to* clean the house since we really *should* have Grandma over for dinner this weekend."

I Can't, I Should, I Have To!

Here are some other "shoulds" and "have-to's"…

- ❏ I have to work extra or the boss will fire me.
- ❏ I have to help out at school or they'll think I'm a terrible mother.
- ❏ I really should get her a present, even though I don't feel like it.
- ❏ I have to go home for the holidays, even though it's usually a disaster.
- ❏ I should clean the house before my husband comes home.

Have you ever thought about what might happen if you didn't do something you "should" for once? What about those Christmases when you go home and each year it's a family disaster? Your stress level mounts as the holiday grows nearer. By Christmas Day itself, your blood pressure begins to climb. You know your dad is just waiting for the perfect time to attack your husband because he's not liked his long hair since the day you got married 25 years ago. By the time the turkey is served, the slings and arrows are flying at full force, and you can't even eat because your ulcer has reacted to the tension in the room, thick enough to cut with the electric knife just used to carve the turkey. Why do you do this to yourself every year? Did you ever have fun, or is the I Should Boxx just trapping you year after year? The punishment you receive and the additional guilt that goes with it are a result of you not taking care of yourself first. Eventually you pay a price, either emotionally or physically.

This year, instead of saying, "I really *should* go home for Christmas" and beating yourself up again, take a risk and get out of that confining, torturous, painful boxx and take care of you and your family first. Plan a Christmas vacation in the tropics, or on a ski slope, or visit friends in another part of the country. Anything! Just don't stay stuck on the treadmill that is taking you further into pain, guilt, and resentment. You'll have a healthier holiday and maybe your father will ask himself how come you didn't come home this year. Old dogs really can learn new tricks if we teach them!

Not all leaps "Out of the Boxx" need to be this extreme. Start on a small scale, and when the school calls and asks you to be the president of the PTA again this year, instead of telling yourself that you really "should" take the job, take a deep breath and think again. If you've volunteered in that role for years, maybe you "should" let someone else do it for a while! Take care of yourself and be true to *you* so that you can take care of, and love, the others in your life. You really can do that for yourself!

The other danger to the "Should" and "Have-to" Boxxes is that these words may imply that they are not our own ideas. How motivated are you to do something that your boss told you that you "should" do versus something you came up with yourself? Or maybe you have decided to quit smoking because everyone tells you that you should. Does it feel like something you want to do, or something that you are suddenly being required to do?

The power of words is enormous, and we will examine that in greater detail in a later chapter. Suffice it to say that your choice of words impacts your attitudes, behaviors and outcomes.

Listen to the difference in these two statements:

"I *can't* go with you today, because I *have* to work."
"I *don't choose to* go with you today because I *choose* to work instead."

You might feel a bit uncomfortable telling your friend that you choose to work instead of spending time with her, but the truth in our words enables us the freedom to break out of our boxxes and take control of our lives. When we use the excuses of "I Can't, I Should, or I Have To," we are essentially providing ourselves poor excuses for being dishonest with ourselves and others.

Other examples of excuses are time and money. How often have you told someone you can't do something because you "don't have time," or you "can't afford" to do something? The truth of the matter is, time and money are never the real reasons that we don't do things. The bottom line is that we *choose* our priorities in life. We *make time and find the money for things that are important to us!* If your child was kidnapped, wouldn't you drop everything you were doing, *make time,* and scrape up the ransom somehow? Of course, you would. Then it's time to start thinking "Out of the Boxx" about what you really mean when it comes to your priorities in life, and be honest with yourself.

Quit telling yourself you just don't have time to exercise, and start being honest enough with yourself to admit that exercise just really isn't that big a priority in your life. Your honesty will also minimize the guilt you feel every time you drive by the gym after promising yourself time and again you would start working out three times a week on your way home because you really "should" get in shape.

As I was struggling to get my Out of the Boxx seminar business off the ground, I knew it would be important to write a book to explain my philosophy to others. I had all the ideas and chapters laid out in my mind, knew exactly what it would look like, and had lots of stories from my travels ready to tie into my concepts. Fortunately, I already had a writing outlet as I wrote a column I called "Out of the Boxx" for the *Denver Nursing Star* newspaper. Although I wasn't featured weekly, it was a great starting place to get my ideas on paper, not to mention an ego booster each time I saw one in print. I knew that each article would be a starting place for the chapters in my book, but I just didn't know when I would find the time to write it. My days were filled selling advertising for the *Nursing*

Star, writing columns, and busily networking with people in Denver prospecting for clients. I was also taking an advanced sales training course so that I would better know how to present and sell my product. Although I knew a book would be a huge plus, I just didn't know when I would find the time to write it. "I just *can't* fit it in," I kept telling myself. "I just don't know where I'll find the time."

Well, one day I met a wonderful man by the name of Joe Sabah. I attended his seminar called, "How to Speak for Fun and Profit." Joe is in his seventies and seemed to know everything about speaking and writing, and I listened with bated breath to every word he said during that talk. Of all the things I was frantically taking notes about, Joe said something that turned on a light bulb in my head. He stressed how important it was to have something to send home with people at our seminars — a book, a CD, a tape – anything to help them keep our important messages close to their hearts and to be able to reflect upon them later. I agreed, but kept scratching my head as to how I could find the time.

He talked about making tapes of our speeches, getting them transcribed, and with ten speeches on ten different subjects we would have a book in no time – in as little as two weeks! I was speechless. The idea of writing a book in two weeks had never occurred to me. The time involved had seemed overwhelming before, but that one little statement suddenly got me thinking "Out of the Boxx," and I knew that I had to change my priorities. I had to put the book first, no matter what, for without it, my progress would be dramatically slowed.

About the same time, my college-aged daughter had called me to catch up about all that was going on in her busy life, and began telling me about a big paper she had due for one of her classes at school. The project sounded huge to me, and although I could sense her stress about getting it all done in time and producing a quality product, I also knew that she

I Can't, I Should, I Have To!

would get it done. She always did. It brought back some of my own college memories of homework and deadlines. I remembered how each project had always felt overwhelming when I first faced it, but how I always completed them by the required deadline. I realized I simply needed to look at my book project as if it were a school assignment. I needed to break it up in segments in my mind, begin with an outline, and start attacking each piece from there. I also needed a deadline, so I chose a date which seemed challenging but reachable, and then I sent out a letter to my two best friends telling them of my plan and requesting that they hold me accountable to my goals. I promised them (in writing) that each Monday morning I would send copies of whatever work I had completed the previous week. Then I jumped in with both feet.

I made the commitment to make that book more important than calling prospects, researching potential radio shows, going out with friends, riding my horses – everything. Two days after Joe's seminar, I sat down at my computer and went to work. For me, the wee hours of the night are when I do my best work. (Don't expect the same thing of me at 5 or 6 a.m. – trust me!) I began with the table of contents at 11 p.m. Friday night, jumping from there into the first chapter, and finally forced myself to go to bed at 3 a.m. Even then, my brain was wild with ideas and I tossed and turned half the night, getting up at 8:30 and starting to write again by 9:30.

My restless night in bed made me think of the five-year-old child on Christmas Eve. I wasn't lying awake all night worrying about stuff. Rather, I couldn't wait to start writing again the next morning! The possibilities awaited me and I could barely contain myself! I worked almost every waking moment that weekend, and 48 hours after I had begun, I had completed the table of contents and the first five chapters, including one round of editing! It was amazing!

You see, I really DID have time to write this book, but I had to make it a priority! I dedicated that Mother's Day weekend to me and my excitement of writing a book that had been screaming to get out for ten months! By putting this project on the top of my priority list, the first draft was completed in three weeks!

What have you been putting off because you "just don't have the time?" How might your life change if you made those things a priority?

In this fast-paced society, it can be as simple as making time for your children. I think the men in our culture get especially sucked into the belief that their roles as providers and breadwinners come first and foremost, and as long as they keep the family in good financial shape, their priorities are straight. Yet, how many of our children are not getting enough quality time with their parents because they "just don't have enough time?"

Jenny

My friend Jenny dreamed of being a nurse, but got pregnant right out of high school and had a second child only a few years later. The bills added up quickly and she and her husband both worked full-time to try to keep up with their financial obligations. What they didn't realize was that they got sucked up on the American treadmill, as so many others do. Years later, Jenny still really wanted to be a nurse, but without her husband's support, she couldn't juggle childcare and work, as well as attend school part-time. Yet, what if they had found a way to make nursing school a priority for her? How would their lives be different? Certainly, Jenny's income would be higher. The nursing shortage in the United States is at epidemic proportions and salaries and benefits have only escalated. What if they had worked out a plan for daycare, carpooling, and juggling household responsibilities? For four years they could have tightened their belts and done without for the short term, or perhaps taken out a loan, so that things might have been better for all of them over the long haul. In

I Can't, I Should, I Have To!

their case, they took the "safe" route of the known, and fell into the Boxx of Not Enough Time.

Mary

Yet, another family in similar circumstances chose a different route. They made one family member's dream a reality by changing their routine and making her a priority. They did not accept the excuse of "we just don't have time."

When I attended nursing school years ago, there was a rather unusual student in my class – at least unusual for the 1970s. Mary was 46 years old and the mother of seven children. She told me she never really planned to have seven children, but that's what God had blessed her with, and she loved every one of them. However, when her youngest finally hit first grade she decided it was time for her to make time for her own needs, and so she came up with a plan. They held a family meeting and decided if they all helped out Mom could go back to school and get her nursing degree. To make life even more complicated, the school was 50 miles away from home and nursing students had to be on the hospital floor by 6:30 a.m. Some nights she just stayed with friends who would let her crash on their couches so she didn't have to get up at 4 a.m. to drive the fifty miles to the hospital.

She told me about some of the ways the family organized their unique system without Mom at the helm. First of all, each child old enough to cook was assigned one night to make dinner. They were also responsible for getting their ingredients put on the weekly grocery list so there were no last-minute trips to the store. The oldest kids were in charge of making lunches for everyone in the morning, and Dad rearranged his work schedule, in order to carpool the kids, to and from school. Laundry and house cleaning duties were divvied up amongst everyone. She was also proud to tell me – "We just gave up ironing completely." The final requirement? Flexibility.

Get Out of Your Boxx

When Mary graduated with the rest of us youngsters, her family was more proud of her than she was, and they were proud of themselves for helping make her dream come true! In addition, she was guaranteed a career that would always provide a good income and job stability. No one in that household was allowed to use the excuse of "I can't." What a great role model she was for her children!

The Boxxes of "I Can't," "I Should," "I Have To," and "I Don't Have Time," are all very confining traps that allow us to lie to ourselves and others in our lives. Don't let these boxxes control your life! Recognize them. Listen to your words and choose them carefully, remembering the power that they have to free you or to confine you!

Then, whenever you're inclined to say "I can't," remember the incredible sights I discovered in the deep, dark ocean because I took a risk and bit my tongue long enough to stop saying "I can't." What can you uncover if you Get Out of Your Boxx too?

"Life comes in CANS, not in cannots."
Jeffrey Mayer

Chapter 6
Boxxed In By Your Past

I was very lucky growing up. I lived in a small town in rural Wisconsin where crime was nearly non-existent and safety seemed as much a given as milk and cheese and Holstein cows. The weekly newspaper focused mostly on general topics of interest like the weather, who go married or celebrated an anniversary, or had a new baby. Of course, if someone in town had gone on a big vacation, their pictures were in the paper as well, taken in whatever scenic locale they had visited. There were no mass murders or gang violence or rapes to write about. The most excitement came from the small state university that, besides farming, was the only real industry of any size in the community. The only other activities worth gossiping about were the occasional fraternity parties and, of course, Homecoming festivities.

There were three stop lights, a handful of police officers, a one-screen movie theatre, three grade schools, one junior high school, and a high school with about 700 students. Everyone knew everyone else — which was a plus as well as a minus. It was a plus because kids always felt safe anywhere they went. There was always someone who knew their mom or dad and would help them out if they needed it. It was a minus because everybody knew everybody else's business.

I will always remember one beautiful spring afternoon when I decided to walk home from high school instead of taking the school bus. It was about a three-mile walk, but I wanted to wander through the two blocks of small shops on the way home and see if there was something I wanted to buy. I also stopped at the bakery where I bought a brownie and carton of milk to enjoy during the rest of the walk home.

What took me by complete surprise when I arrived home were my mother's first words to me. Without skipping a beat as I walked in the door she said, "I hear you stopped in at the bakery on your way home!" Talk about Big Brother! Living in a small town is its own unique experience!

Yet, it was this same environment that formed the choices I made as I lived through my teenage years. I was the ultimate "Goody Two Shoes." I never picked up a cigarette, got drunk, took drugs, or got into any kind of trouble for fear that the "network" would have delivered the news to my parents before I even got home! Hilary Clinton writes that it "Takes a Village to Raise a Child." It's too bad we don't have more villages today.

I came from a family of hard working, conservative folks who had lived through the Great Depression and, as a result, had incredible respect for the dollar. They taught us to work hard, save our money, respect other people and their property, be polite, and always do our best. "Anything worth doing, is worth doing right," still rings in my ears. We had enough money to be comfortable, go on vacations, have a modest home, and never want for anything – although extravagance was not part of our lifestyle.

As the youngest of four children, I had it made. My older sister was married and my oldest brother went off to the Navy by the time I was nine, leaving me with one remaining teenaged brother, and even he was gone by the time I was 12. Those last years I was essentially an only child and was fortunate enough to be able to spend more time with my parents than my siblings had. I was basically a happy kid, and if I had to measure it, I would say that 95 percent of my childhood was wonderful. Feeling safe and loved, doing well in school, being respected by my teachers and ministers were all great self-esteem builders. Girl Scouts, swimming in the lake, and going to Dairy Queen on a Saturday night are memories I will cherish forever.

I developed strong self-esteem, confidence, trust, strength, character, compassion, leadership skills, intelligence, and the freedom to do many things. But I also had a negative experience that locked me into a terrifying Boxx of Fear.

I was sexually abused.

I never told ANYONE about this experience for 20 years. It was my deep, dark secret. The perpetrator was a person in a position of trust who moved out of the area shortly after and kept the secret to himself as well. He knew that victims of abuse, especially children, are afraid to tell anyone about what happened to them for fear of being punished or blamed for the event in some way. I'm sure he didn't spend a great deal of time worrying about being discovered. Yet, as was predictable, I felt responsible for everything to do with the situation. I felt guilty, dirty, bad, and downright shameful.

I was 13 years old.

For most of my adult life I felt as though I must be the only one who felt the way I did. Little did I know that one in three girls and one in six boys are molested by the time they are 18 years old.[i] I was hardly alone.

It wasn't until I was 43 years old that I told my mother about what happened to me, and it took all my courage to do so. (My father had already passed away by that time.) The lifelong feelings of guilt made me fear she would blame me for the situation, or reject me as "damaged goods." (Believe it or not, some parents do react this way, much to the detriment of their children – even grown children.) My mother was the

Get Out of Your Boxx

Rock of Gibraltar for me, and her reaction helped my healing more than she will ever know. She cried with me, held me, loved me, and unconditionally accepted me, which was all I was seeking, even 30 years after it happened.

I believe I was more fortunate than many who have suffered childhood sexual abuse. The 95 percent of my childhood that had been rock solid and built upon a foundation of trust, caring, and love helped dilute the five percent which had been terrifying and painful. Although I was left with life-long scars that locked me into several boxxes for years, it could have been so much worse. For example, I still get stuck in the Claustrophobia Boxx periodically as a direct result of that frightening experience. I swore to myself that I would never be trapped again, and I am always subconsciously aware of my surroundings. I know where the doors are in any room, and small crowded places still make me anxious.

I have spent much time living in many other boxxes related to this incident, but the most important thing I recognize is that I am a survivor. Not only did I find a way to escape my terror so many years ago, I have since found a way to make peace with the experience and to find a way to give it meaning and perspective in my life.

Is there something in your life that has left you Boxxed in by Your Past?

Many different experiences can leave people with deep scars and painful memories. Some of these are obvious issues like abuse. Larger tragedies like the shootings at Columbine High School, or the attack on the World Trade Center on September 11 left many people affected in various ways. Others may seem relatively minor by comparison. Yet, it is the *perception* left upon the victim that holds him captive. The memories may be large or extremely small but they leave an indelible imprint, none the less. Events from your past need not only have occurred in your childhood, they may have occurred in adulthood. Perhaps you lost your job and are still reeling from shock and denial. Or living through the pain of divorce may have left you doubting your ability to love and be loved. Even something as common as being in a car accident may have left you unsettled and anxious just driving down the road.

See if any of these examples strike a chord with you, and might lead you to investigate the Boxxes of Your Past that may keep you from reaching your full potential. These are not all "bad" things. Some may just be everyday life situations, yet they may hold special significance for you. You may also think of many more yourself by remembering your own experiences and those of your friends you grew up with.

- ❑ Neglect or abuse
  (Sexual, physical, verbal, or emotional)
- ❑ Being ignored or given the "silent treatment"
- ❑ Not having enough money
- ❑ Being a child of a minister or public figure
- ❑ Name calling – by adults or children
- ❑ Living with a perfectionist
- ❑ Bullying from classmates or teachers
- ❑ Being "different" from your peers in some way
- ❑ Losing a loved one
- ❑ Being too fat, too thin, too tall, or too short
- ❑ Having a lengthy illness, whether life threatening or not
- ❑ Parents divorced
- ❑ Losing a job or other significant opportunity
- ❑ Living with an alcoholic, whether as an adult or a child
- ❑ Being uprooted because of a family move or moving many times
- ❑ Witnessing a stressful event

- ☐ Being perceived as either a "Goody Two Shoes" or the opposite — a "Troublemaker."
- ☐ Parents frequently absent (Physically or emotionally)
- ☐ Parents not comfortable showing love
- ☐ Living in an environment of highly competitive people
- ☐ Parent with a career in the military

You may already know precisely which life experiences have left you boxxed in. If so, have hope. You don't have to stay locked in those boxxes forever. There are ways to break down those walls. The important thing is recognition and understanding. Putting things into perspective with some sort of meaning can help your wounds heal and allow your beliefs about yourself to grow and change.

By choosing *not* to do something to break down the walls of your boxxes, or by ignoring your past completely, you may be holding yourself back in a variety of ways: Perhaps in how you relate to other people, in getting ahead in your career, in meeting your goals, or maybe in your own beliefs about your self-worth. Unfortunately, it may also be affecting your physical health as well.

The behaviors and symptoms of living in the Boxx of Your Past are as varied as the experiences that may have put you there.

You may:
- ☐ Be angry
- ☐ Feel sad or depressed
- ☐ Be extremely competitive
- ☐ Be chronically tired
- ☐ Act shy or withdrawn
- ☐ Be aggressive
- ☐ Have low self-esteem

- ❏ Fear certain situations or environments
- ❏ Be impatient
- ❏ Dislike or fear certain kinds of people
- ❏ Run away from conflict
- ❏ Be the class clown, always entertaining everyone
- ❏ Dig your heels in and fight
- ❏ Yell at your children or others
- ❏ Be perfectionistic
- ❏ Be critical of others
- ❏ Feel uncomfortable in crowds
- ❏ Be a pessimist
- ❏ Feel uncomfortable talking in front of people
- ❏ Hate to be alone
- ❏ Be a procrastinator
- ❏ Be an organizational nightmare or slob
- ❏ Always want to be in control of situations
- ❏ Never feel comfortable taking risks
- ❏ Sleep a lot
- ❏ Not able to concentrate easily
- ❏ Be reckless or take too many risks
- ❏ Have an addiction
- ❏ Feel responsible for everyone else
- ❏ Feel uncomfortable if you don't have consistent routine in your life
- ❏ Spend money too freely or not feel comfortable spending it at all
- ❏ Become defensive easily

By recognizing these types of behaviors, can you see where they might be holding you back from finding the many possibilities awaiting you? How might they be limiting you from attaining things that you really want? Some of these responses may reflect small issues in your life, while others may impose enormous limitations.

- ❑ Perhaps you don't feel comfortable taking risks, so you would never consider taking a vacation out of the country. Can you imagine the beautiful, far-off places you might miss?
- ❑ Maybe you have a hard time concentrating and would really like to return to school for an advanced degree, but the thought of studying seems impossible to you since you know that focusing will be difficult.
- ❑ It could be that your shyness is limiting you from asking for the raise that you feel you deserve and thus deteriorates your self-esteem even further.
- ❑ Might it be that your chronic fatigue is holding you back from having another child because you fear that you won't have enough energy to care for a second baby?
- ❑ Could your defensiveness be keeping you from making new friends or finding love?
- ❑ Are your frequent shopping sprees keeping you on the workaholic treadmill, just trying to stay out of debt?

The Boxx of Your Past has far-reaching effects when you consider some of the results. Yet, recognizing that the walls are breakable can free you to move forward. Facing your past can be scary. However, if you knew there was light at the end of the tunnel, wouldn't it be worth it?

What finally helped me on my journey was realizing several things. Most importantly, I stopped looking at the tragic events in my past as if they were a punishment, or simply that life wasn't fair, and decided to find a reason for them. As I thought about it over time, I finally found a way to put it all into a perspective that had meaning for me. I decided that God didn't just "allow" the abuse to happen to me, but that it was a life lesson He gave me. That may sound confusing at first, but if I hadn't lived through that experience, I wouldn't be as compassionate and empathetic as I am today. I remember being a pretty strong, dominant kid and I still have many of those qualities, but I also have a softer side to my personality as a result. That is the sensitive part of me, the one who was first drawn towards nursing to help people. Maybe helping the helpless was therapeutic and healing for me because at the time I was abused I didn't feel anyone was there to help me.

Those experiences are also part of the backbone of what my motivational company is about. When I discovered the statistics regarding sexually abused children in this country, I realized that part of my journey was also to share my survival story with them. Perhaps my pain and recovery will aid in the healing of another. I have begun to look at each experience in my life now as a "life lesson." It makes them less frightening and so much more thought provoking.

My friend Jenna and I were having a discussion a while back about good and evil and religion. I told her I believe that everything has a lesson attached to it and that it is up to us to figure out the lesson. Sometimes they are easy and sometimes they are involved and take a long time to discover. While she didn't argue about the concept itself, she felt more comfortable believing that evil just exists in the world, and sometimes bad things just happen to people and that God is there to help us cope afterwards. While I agreed that God is there to help get us through difficult times, I told her I was much more comfortable knowing that if something bad happened to me, it was a life lesson for me versus the idea that evil could just jump out and grab me at any moment just because I was in the wrong place at the wrong time. This is the perspective that seems to work for me – it isn't necessarily for everyone.

However, when I look at the incredible goodness that has resulted from some terrible events, I find peace with this philosophy. Mothers Against Drunk Driving (MADD) formed as a result of terrible drinking and driving accidents that took the lives of so many young people. Look at the accomplishments of this incredible organization since its inception. The tragic losses of September 11 brought our nation together as no other time since Pearl Harbor. A forest fire that wiped out thousands of acres of forestland in Yellowstone National Park several years ago now yields new growth and possibilities for a healthier forest.

My perspective helps me deal with the Boxxes of My Past, and helps me break free of the limitations they held over me. If you can find a philosophy and perspective that makes your past events make some sense to you, then you can break down your walls too.

Remember, the past is the past and you have already survived it.

It has made you who you are but only to whatever degree you let it. Anthony Robbins reminds us that, "The past is not the future."

It is easy to become a victim of your past and let it hold you in its grip for the rest of your life. Once again, look around you at people you know. You will quickly recognize those who are morbidly stuck in the Victim Boxx. Nothing is ever their fault. Life is unfair. They believe they are this way because their parents didn't love them or their boyfriend left them or their boss doesn't appreciate them. They have all the excuses and none of the solutions. They are stuck in their boxx and they have no intention of doing anything about it because they keep waiting for someone else to solve everything for them, and they continue to be hurt and confused when no one does. They are eternal pessimists. In fact, they have the pure, unadulterated talent of bringing everyone else around them down to their level. If things aren't going well for them, they certainly are not going to help anyone else succeed either. There is also a "payoff" for being a victim – they never have to take accountability or responsibility for themselves or their actions. It's an easy excuse for absolutely anything that doesn't go right in their lives. Yet, they are so stuck in their comfy "Victim Boxxes" they can't see beyond its walls.

The Boxx of Your Past does not have to hold you hostage. Decide to leave it in the past – learn from it, embrace it, and use it to grow. It can be a catalyst for much greater things to come.

"Create meaning to your suffering."
Viktor Frakl, survivor of a Nazi death camp

Chapter 7
The Oh-So-Perfect Boxx

Perfectionism is a way of life for some. Personally, if I'm having brain surgery, you can bet I want a surgeon who does not have the work ethic, "OK, that's good enough!" As far as I'm concerned, he or she had better be attentive to each and every meticulous detail! Perhaps a bit less life and death, but equally important, are other professions where I want someone who is detail oriented — my accountant, my lawyer, or the mechanic who services the planes I fly on, to name a few. Certainly, when I am signing an important contract involving some aspect of my life, I want a perfectionist professional guiding me in dotting all the i's and crossing all the t's!

While these specific professions require perfectionistic tendencies, might there be a down side to living in this particular boxx? Perhaps for those actually stuck in the Boxx of Perfectionism, the cost doesn't seem high, or even apparent. However, for the significant others in the lives of these seemingly "faultless" people, the cost may take a huge toll. The expectations that the perfectionist has for himself are one thing, but they can easily set unrealistically high expectations for others, and then become critical if those standards are not met.

Perfectionism usually begins at an early age when a child is raised in an environment of constant criticism and/or where high behavioral expectations are the norm. To avoid the pain of being chastised or unaccepted, he learns to go over-

The Oh-So-Perfect Boxx

board in making sure that everything is perfect. The more perfect his performance, the better his odds of receiving acceptance, love, and approval — or so he believes. By taking extreme measures to avoid mistakes, he soon adopts the pattern of perfectionism. At the same time he often learns to be motivated by fear of failure rather than be driven by the thrill of success. He also begins to believe that others value him for his performance and achievements, and not necessarily for the person he is. His self-esteem is shaky, at best, as acceptance is closely tied to performance. Thus, he begins a vicious cycle of setting high, unattainable standards for himself. Then he worries about what might happen if he is not successful. When he doesn't reach the perfect level of performance, his inner self-talk reminds him harshly that he truly is a failure, and that he must try even harder the next time. Just one more hole in his fragile shell of self-esteem, confirming his underlying belief that he is worthless.

Most of us want to do our best and expect others will do the same in return. A housekeeper who does a great job cleaning hotel rooms is a valued employee, especially if she can work efficiently as well. But if that same housekeeper were a perfectionist and spent endless hours on minute details, she would cost her employer both time and money. He would have angry guests waiting to check in at the lobby while their rooms were still being cleaned, and his cleaning budget would skyrocket.

As with all the other boxxes, this one has its place. However, doing a good job versus being a perfectionist are two different things. Remember back to that protective Boxx of Body Armor that can help you? Being a great employee is one thing. Being a perfect employee is unrealistic.

So what happens when the Perfectionistic Boxx gets out of control? It can affect those same three areas I mentioned before: your career, your relationships, and your health. The cleaning lady in the previous example could lose her job if she can't clean more efficiently. A wife might throw in the towel on her marriage after spending years trying to keep her house clean enough for her husband who may never find it quite good enough. An executive may develop a bleeding ulcer worrying about the possibility of delivering less-than-perfect proposals for each presentation. Worst of all, the vicious cycle of perfectionism can be perpetuated from one generation to the next, as children learn from their parents what the parents originally learned from their own parents. When does it stop?

Not being a perfectionist myself (I tend to fall more towards the "messy housekeeper" personality), I didn't have a personal angle to share regarding this boxx. But I have a close friend who agreed to let me use him as my example.

George

George is a 40-year-old divorced man and knows that he is an extreme perfectionist. His friends tease him about his behaviors and he takes their jokes in stride. His house, truck, and garage are meticulous. His body is in perfect shape. He has a precise exercise program that involves a one-hour run EVERY day, and he has run without fail for over 20 years. The only two days he missed were when his daughter was born, and when he was so sick he literally couldn't get out of bed. The local newspaper has even written a story about him, calling him "The Running Man," as he is a landmark in his community, traveling his same route each day. He mows his lawn at the same time each week. His day is almost a science of time and organization. His career is one that demands detailed cleaning of precision equipment involved in food processing and he must pass scrupulous inspections by the Food and Drug Administration or his company can face serious fines. Needless to say, his bosses love him as they can always count on him to meet the high industrial standards.

As I was teasing him about his habits one day, he told me a funny story, which made us both laugh, but also let me realize that he was starting to chip away at his perfectionist boxx, little by little. (Remember, recognition is the first step.) He told me that every morning after breakfast, one of his self-imposed, mandatory chores was to vacuum the carpet. (He claims it only takes six minutes.) At first, he couldn't really tell me why he feels obligated to do this daily. Certainly he likes things clean. But then he confessed something else – he said he loves to see the lines in the carpet left by the vacuum cleaner! OK, so this may seem a little unusual, but as long as he is not hurting anyone, what's the problem? Well, then he admitted to me that he used to yell at his young daughter for walking on the carpet and messing up the lines! At that point, his boxx had gone way beyond affecting only him, and had branched out to his innocent child who was taking hits on her own developing self-esteem for exhibiting perfectly normal behavior.

Fortunately he had begun to recognize this boxx and has learned to take it on as "his" issue and not inflict his expectations upon everyone else. Although he still "needs" to vacuum every morning, he and his daughter now joke about his vacuuming exploits, and she takes special joy in making "snow angels" in the carpet to purposefully destroy the carpet lines! They can laugh together about his need to be neat and he has learned that it's important for her to be a kid!

Is living in the Boxx of Perfectionism working for or against you? Ask yourself these questions:

- ❏ Are you highly competitive?
- ❏ Do you think other people achieve their success easily and you have to work hard to do the same?
- ❏ Do you short yourself on sleep, staying up all hours to check and recheck your work?
- ❏ Do you get frustrated when others don't do things "your way"?

- ❑ Do you make a big deal about things other people seem to consider minor issues?
- ❑ Do you feel tense and restless if things aren't perfect in your home or work environment?
- ❑ Do you feel like you never have enough time for fun because you're always too busy with chores you "have to do"?
- ❑ Do you ever feel like you spend all your time doing things for everyone else and never have any time left for yourself?
- ❑ Do you ever feel like others don't care enough to do a good job?
- ❑ Do you feel like a failure if you don't do something perfectly?
- ❑ Do you "beat yourself up" if you make a mistake?
- ❑ Do you get angry at yourself if you don't finish everything on your "to do" list?
- ❑ Do you feel most comfortable when you perform your regular routines?
- ❑ Do you feel uneasy trying new things?
- ❑ Do you feel uncomfortable delegating jobs to others, as you fear they either won't get done, or they won't get done right?

These are just some examples of behaviors that might indicate that you are trapped in the Boxx of Perfectionism. Let's look at how a few more detailed examples can cost you or your loved ones more than you might realize.

You Are Highly Competitive

Perfectionists are frequently very competitive since they are always striving to be the best. However, the pressure they put upon their children can lead to increased feelings of stress and anxiety in the child. The overly competitive "soccer parent" personality has become so prevalent these days it's no wonder children feel stress at very early ages. These pressures may make a child afraid to try lest he or she might fail, causing the parent disappointment. Some kids eventually quit competitive sports to avoid the possibility of displeasing their parents if they don't perform well enough. Children then lose the opportunity to learn that failing is not the end of the world, and that many lessons can be learned from failure. It may also cheat the child out of opportunities to grow and excel in a sport he might have otherwise learned to love.

You Don't Feel Comfortable Delegating

Delegating a job to someone else implies that you trust them enough to get the job done. When you aren't comfortable delegating to your employees or family members, they might take it as a sign that you don't trust them. When people don't feel trusted, they don't trust in return. If you want your child or spouse to trust you, you must show them trust as well. Start by giving them small tasks so they can experience success, which also allows you to see how they handle the responsibility. In addition, by delegating to others, you free yourself from added tasks on your own "to do" list, thus giving yourself more time for you AND your family.

Are You Uncomfortable Trying New Things?

Many perfectionists are uncomfortable trying new things because it always involves taking a risk, and thus, their fear of failure rears its ugly head. Staying within their "safe" routine and environment makes them more comfortable as they believe they are more likely to achieve success in their known territory. Yet, by remaining in the known, they may be missing out on countless possibilities of excitement, learning, and enjoyment. Going on vacation to Mexico, for example, could be a great cultural experience for the perfectionist and his children, but the risks of possibly facing a new challenge for which he may not have an easy answer sounds much more frightening.

Making A Mistake

Perfectionists are afraid of making a mistake more than almost anything. Mistakes prove they are not perfect. Their deeply seated childhood need for love makes them fear that others will stop loving them if their imperfections are revealed. Yet, what they don't realize is that when they act so perfect that no one can live up to them, they actually push people away. In addition, they don't understand that by making mistakes, they can learn valuable lessons. One of the most obvious examples of that is the 3M Post-It Note. It was actually a huge mistake – it was originally designed to be a glue that would hold forever, but it failed miserably. The unexpected result was a product that is now sold the world over and has become a household word. Mistakes can create successes, but the perfectionist who fears making mistakes more than anything is missing opportunities each and every day he stays in his Perfectionist Boxx trying to avoid making mistakes.

Remember my friend who vacuums for only six minutes every day? Well, six minutes a day adds up to over 36 *hours a year!* What might he and his daughter do that would be fun, memorable, rewarding, and loving with an extra 36 hours, instead of vacuuming the carpet every day just to see the lines and to reassure himself that his house is perfectly clean? The sad thing is that he has really lied to himself about what his real priorities are. By convincing himself that he feels better by vacuuming his carpet every day, he is closing the door to many of life's great possibilities!

Learning to accept each other's behaviors as part of who we are is crucial to good communications and relationships. At the same time, recognizing when your boxxes are inhibiting you from living your life to the fullest is a key in YOU becoming the most magnificent person you can possibly be.

The Oh-So-Perfect Boxx

Study the Boxx of Perfectionism carefully, remembering that it is deeply rooted in the overriding Boxx of Fear. Ask yourself what you are afraid of and what would happen if you allowed yourself to fail occasionally?

Set yourself up to fail on a small scale. Or force yourself to change your routine for a day and see if anyone notices. You might surprise yourself and discover something new that you never imagined was possible!

"Don't get in the habit of enjoying the problem more than doing something about it."
Coach Rachelle Disbennet-Lee, MCC, MS

Chapter 8
Workaholism And The Wrong Career — The Treadmill Boxxes

Do you wish you had more time to spend with your family? Keep hoping for more sleep every night? Need to reignite the flame with your spouse? Ever pray for "someday" when you're not going to be too busy to enjoy life? All these things are possible ... if you're not stuck in the Boxxes of Workaholism or the Wrong Career.

OK, so you're not 17 anymore. You can't sleep until noon, party all night and spend every weekend skiing like you did back when time seemed endless and responsibilities belonged to someone else. You grew up and became a responsible, productive member of society. With two kids in college, a mortgage, car payments, a huge balance on your credit cards, and your upcoming family vacation to Disney World, you need every dollar you can get. You have to work your tail off to keep your head above water – right?

Well, you are not alone in this belief. The American culture has rewarded us for this type of thinking and sometimes even gives extra rewards to those who dedicate most of their lives to their career. Big business knows how to prey on our cultural values and behaviors that support materialism and competitiveness. In addition, many employees get locked into a career that may not fulfill their personal needs but pads their wallets and provides a retirement plan. These deadly traps can lead to the "hamster on the wheel syndrome" – going around

The Treadmill Boxxes

and around and around, doing the same thing day after day with no end in sight. Getting up every morning, going to work, spending the day at the office, fighting traffic, going home exhausted, racing to the kids' soccer game, ordering a pizza, falling into a heap in front of the TV, and going to bed, only to wake up and start the same routine again the next day. The only possible hope for change is the upcoming weekend when it's time to recharge your batteries and prepare to start the whole cycle over again.

The average full-time employee spends 2,000 hours a year at his job. If you are stuck in a job leaving you feeling less than satisfied, ask yourself why? Why do you consciously choose to spend such a big part of your life not enjoying yourself? Why are you missing out on so many things that might excite you and inspire you to leap out of bed every morning anticipating the many possibilities awaiting you? What are you waiting for?

You pay a huge price when you get stuck in the Boxxes of the Wrong Career or Workaholism. Divorce, high blood pressure, heart disease, and visits to psychologists each year are higher now than at any time in our country's history. The statistics are frightening. Money spent on these issues alone could probably feed the world's hungry. Many people keep trying to find a way to get off the treadmill and find balance, but for most it continues to remain an elusive concept.

I believe that all boxxes start out as "Body Armor," keeping you safe within your environment. When it comes to work and a career, you first develop the Responsible Employee Boxx, which is good. This protective boxx develops as you grow up and join the adult world and get your first job, whether that's babysitting, lawn mowing or delivering newspapers. You begin to learn how to plan your life around your work schedule, how to dress the part, how to be reliable, and to be committed to a job and be part of a team.

You probably hit some unpleasant experiences along

the way that taught you additional lessons in the construction of your boxx. For example, if you did a poor job mowing your neighbor's lawn and they asked the kid down the block to do it next time, you learned a lesson about quality work. If you came to work late and took too many breaks at your first job at Taco Bell, you may not have received the raise you were hoping for, or perhaps you got fired. These valuable lessons from the "school of hard knocks" helped prepare you for the "grown-up" career world, and you began to develop your Body Armor Boxx to keep you safe. You learned to show up on time, be polite to customers, and do everything that was asked of you – even if you didn't necessarily like it. Ideally, you became accountable for your actions, worked hard, gave of yourself, and went home feeling as though you had accomplished something, and were valued by your employer.

As a consumer you also learned important information required in constructing your career foundation. You started to recognize what good service looked like and, hopefully, how to give it to others. You began to believe in giving your best because you hoped that others would give you their best in return. All these and other behaviors became significant building blocks in your Responsible Worker Boxx, no matter where you went or what type of work you were in. They were qualities to be proud of and earned your employer's respect and praise.

Workaholism

The Responsible Worker Boxx has the sneaky ability to develop into the Workaholic Boxx without you even realizing it. It can become a never-ending treadmill that may take you on a ride from which there is seemingly no escape. Ask yourself these questions:

Do you
- ❏ Dread going to work every day?
- ❏ Spend more than 50 hours a week there?

The Treadmill Boxxes

- ❏ Miss your children's events because you just "can't get away?"
- ❏ Feel like a hamster on a wheel, going around endlessly, without seeing light at the end of the tunnel?

Then maybe your Responsible Worker Boxx has overgrown into the one called Workaholism.

If you are a health care worker, policeman, fireman, or other public service provider, it is especially easy to get talked into working extra shifts when you know the clients will be shortchanged if you don't stay. Being a caring person is what brought you into this type of career in the first place, so saying no to people in need just isn't in your character and may lead to feelings of guilt. Yet, sometimes saying no is necessary to keep both your physical and mental health balanced, and your clients safer.

Years ago I was head nurse of a premature intensive care nursery. I had enough nurses on staff in the unit to accommodate a certain number of critically ill infants on any given day. Since we could never predict how many sick babies would be in the unit each day, staffing was based on a rule of averages. That meant some days we had too many nurses and some days, not enough. It was strictly a numbers game driven by the budget. While most of the time this system allowed for adequate patient care, the odds were that at some time there just weren't going to be enough nurses to go around. When those days occurred, the drill was for management to beg, plead, and cajole every nurse to work whatever extra shifts they possibly could. Overtime pay was a big incentive to some, and frequently covered the shortages temporarily. However, during times of prolonged peak census, the fatigue level started to show and even bonus pay or promises for extra vacation days were not enough to entice nurses to work longer hours.

Get Out of Your Boxx

As manager, I was on salary so overtime didn't apply to me. However, I frequently battled my own feelings of guilt concerning the possibility that some baby might not get adequate care due to short staffing. At the same time I also had ulterior motives: I hoped that if I made a good enough impression on my supervisors, by doing my fair share of extras, I may have a chance for a promotion at some point in my career. Stuck between these two issues, I got sucked into staying and working extra shifts quite often.

I will always remember one particular day when the unit was especially busy and premature twins and triplets seemed to be dropping from the sky. I agreed to stay *again* and was caring for an extremely critical infant whose odds of survival were about 50/50 at best. It was important to be sharp and have my wits about me as the slightest changes were significant, and could be life threatening. As it turned out, I cared for that baby for 20 hours straight, stopping only to eat and take bathroom breaks. Looking back, I thank God I didn't make any mistakes that day. My fatigue level certainly affected my reflexes, my assessment skills, and my judgment at some point during that shift, which could have easily risked the life of that child. I was lucky. The child did fine.

Yet, wouldn't I have been smarter in the long run to stand my ground and say no to management, which would have resulted in some babies being sent to another hospital with better staffing? We could have avoided taking the risk altogether. Between my inherent caring nature and my need for recognition, I may have taken a very unnecessary risk. As it turned out, my hope for recognition wasn't even realized! My supervisor hadn't even known that I had stayed, much less worked a 20-hour shift, as she had already moved on to the next staffing crisis. So much for my ego and promotion possibility! I risked my license, my health, my self-esteem, and the baby's care, for nothing.

And what price did my family pay? I was overtired and

cranky when I got home. They missed the time with me, which was justifiably theirs to begin with. The ongoing regularity with which I would step in and work extra shifts caused me to be chronically physically and emotionally stressed out, which ultimately took its toll on me. I quit taking care of myself and as a result, didn't take the best care of my family either. The ultimate realization came to me too late. I got sucked into the Boxx of Workaholism and hadn't even realized it. Eventually, the stress I put upon myself with this job led me to burnout level and I left nursing altogether.

Caregiver careers are not the only paths that can suck you in. There are many others. If you're a competitive corporate climber, keeping up to your colleagues may be all that it takes to make you keep your nose to the grindstone. Don't kid yourself! Your superiors know how to use you to their advantage. The "publish or perish" adage of faculty is yet another well-worn path to the treadmill.

How does the Responsible Worker Boxx develop into one of Workaholism? Let me give you an example. Let's say you're fresh out of college and you've landed your first job in a financial corporation. You have your own cubicle and a 40-hour-a-week job with a week of vacation after your first year, good health benefits, and a salary of $40,000 a year! You couldn't be happier! You're excited about your entry into the grown-up world and you love your job. For a while everything seems great, but after you get settled into your new routine you begin to realize that your manager has it even better. He drives a nicer car, has a larger office, gets more vacation and doesn't seem to have as much mundane work as you do. You think maybe you'd like his job, and you begin to keep your eye on him. You start to emulate him, believing that whatever he did right, you can too. Pretty soon you start staying late to work on extra projects, and after a while you get noticed! Your manager is so pleased with your additional work that he gives you another project and you believe this is your ticket to the

Get Out of Your Boxx

next promotion that comes along. At last, the manager gets promoted and of course, he recommends you to replace him! Your plan worked.

With new responsibilities come greater rewards. They pay you $60,000 a year, you get your own office in the corner with a reasonable view, two weeks vacation, better benefits, and now 20 people report to you! Life is great! You love your job! Then, of course, it starts all over again. You grab the next rung on the ladder and a new BMW is calling you. Plus, by now you have a family and a mortgage. But you're young and ambitious and the responsibilities of management are challenging but interesting, even though you end up taking work home for a couple of hours each evening and a few on the weekends. The extra vacation time is great, and your family loves the new house you can afford. You keep working hard, and now you're putting in 50 hours a week at the office and find yourself staying late every night. But you're where you want to be – right?

Of course, over the years you become vice president of the company, have a six figure income, an office with one of the best views, a Mercedes, four weeks of vacation, a benefit package that covers you for life, and your name is known all over town. You have everything you always dreamed of – and some things you didn't. You're working 75 hours a week. Your stress level has left you with high blood pressure and a mild heart attack. Your wife left you because she said you were never home. You don't really know your children because they were always in bed when you got home and you missed much of what was happening in their lives. You certainly missed more of their soccer games than you saw. The fact is you were always tired, short-tempered, or working when you were home, and they knew it was best to give you space. The boxx you built for yourself kept them out as much as it locked you in.

As you look back, do you have any regrets? If you were

suddenly on your deathbed, would you wish you had spent more time at the office, or more time with your loved ones? What price have you paid for your Boxx of Workaholism? What did your family really want — all those material possessions or more time with you? The other cruel realization is if you did die tomorrow (God forbid), your company would replace you quickly enough. No one is irreplaceable. No one! Despite any thoughts to the contrary.

An unforeseen result of the Boxx of Workaholism comes much later – at retirement. What should be a wonderful time is frequently cut short as many retirees die within the first 18 months of retiring. Why? It is suspected that many individuals define themselves by their job. In other words, without their jobs, they no longer know who they are or what they have to offer. Introducing yourself as "Jim, Chief Executive Officer of the Jones Company," doesn't exactly feel the same as telling someone you *used* to be Chief Executive Officer of the Jones Company. It can be overwhelming, suddenly having to fill empty days, when once you didn't have time to catch your breath. The suicide rate in elderly men is the highest of all age groups.[ii] What price indeed?

The Boxx of Workaholism has been predominately a male territory over the last century, as men in our culture were conditioned to believe they were fulfilling their jobs as fathers and husbands by being good financial providers. Wives and children, however, may be judging the men in their lives by different qualities, such as time and affection. Women now fall prey to this boxx as well, as more and more women work outside the home and in management. In addition, the traditional role of women in our culture still includes that of "mother and caretaker of house and home." Most women over age 40 still have vivid images of June Cleaver, from *Leave It to Beaver*, the television show from the early 1960s. June was the ultimate homemaker with a spotlessly clean house, perfect hairdo, and cookies in the oven when the kids came home from school. So the stress level for women can be even worse, trying to balance both the corporate world and motherly expectations. When both parties in a relationship are workaholics, the costs escalate even further.

How can you climb out of this boxx? First, remember your real priorities. Family and health should be front and center despite what your employer wants you to believe! Remember, if you're not taking care of yourself first, it's hard to take care of anyone else. Schedule time for you and your family and write it on your calendar in ink, the same way you schedule appointments with your clients. Aren't you equally important? Promise your kids that every Friday night they will have 100 percent of your undivided attention. Limit yourself to two hours of work on the weekend. Make sure to get enough sleep so that you don't shortchange yourself physically. Not only will it help you function better at work, you won't be as short tempered with those around you. Realize that working 45 to 50 hours a week as a well-rested, balanced person is a more positive contribution to your job than being a 65-hour-a-week zombie. Examine your finances and consider whether you really need that new boat, sports car, RV or snowmobile. You probably haven't had time to use them anyway.

The Workaholism Boxx is a deadly trap that can be avoided if you recognize it. But just as significant, is the Boxx of the Wrong Career. . .

The Wrong Career Boxx

Finding yourself stuck in the Wrong Career Boxx is just another seemingly inescapable treadmill. You may hate your job, or just not find it challenging or interesting anymore. However, your desire to change always gets outweighed by your fears of taking a risk, fear of failure, fear of success, or just plain laziness. I know people who have held the same job for 30 years and still love going to work every day. My two

The Treadmill Boxxes

pilot friends absolutely love flying. Being in the cockpit of an airplane is *always* exciting to them, and whenever they talk about flying I see the passion in their eyes! What is their biggest frustration? The airlines require mandatory retirement at age 60. They would love to keep flying for as long as possible if they could. Now that's being excited about your job!

By the same token, I know people who have either hated their job since day one, or just don't find it exciting anymore. Yet, day after day off they go "to the mines," as my father used to say. I know nurses who have worked on the same unit with the same types of patients for 40 years. Some still love it every single day, finding excitement with various patients and their different needs and life stories. Yet, there are others who are such miserably unhappy people that they scare the pants off of any new nurse who comes to work there. The patients certainly recognize it too. I think nursing must have created the term "burnout" long before it became common jargon in the rest of the world. Working with people like that, I understand why. They made everyone else around them miserable.

So why would you allow yourself to be miserable for eight hours every day? Yes, I said "allow yourself" to be miserable. For it is all about choices. You can either choose to change, or choose to stay. No one is holding you there – except you!

You might think that in today's economic times, with layoffs affecting hundreds of thousands of people that you may not have the luxury of choosing whatever job you want. While that is somewhat true, I firmly believe that if you want something badly enough, you will find a way. As my friend, Gary Harvey likes to say, "I've heard there's a recession and I've chosen not to take part in it!" He refuses to let outside forces deter him from building a career he loves.

Occasionally a success story carries more weight when it involves someone we know. Have you ever heard the rags-to-riches story of Sylvester Stallone? More than anything, Stallone wanted to be an actor, but everyone told him he was too ugly and coarse to be more than a bit-part actor. So after many rejections for better roles, he came up with a new plan. He decided to write. After many bumps in the road, including a point where he was practically penniless, he wrote the screenplay for *Rocky*. Excited with his product, he began to market the story to several agents, but with one stipulation — that *he* play the lead role of Rocky. Although many liked the story and thought it had a good chance of being successful, they were convinced it would fail with him in the lead. No one wanted to take a risk on an unknown, much less an ugly, coarse unknown actor like Stallone. He was offered huge amounts of money for the script alone but he wanted to act, and had just written the perfect story for a main character who was no Prince Charming. So he stuck to his guns and kept knocking on doors. At last, someone agreed to buy his script and allow him to act, offering him a ridiculously low price for the film. The end result? Not only did he get to act in his own movie, he was nominated for Best Actor and his film was the Academy Award Winner for Best Film in 1976. This man knew what he wanted and didn't take no for an answer. In addition, his career took off in a way that no one could have predicted and he became a multi-millionaire.

Of course, the moral of the story is when you know what you want and you are willing to think "Outside the Boxx," possibilities present themselves to you.

Let's say you've been a secretary all your life and you "wish" you could be a legal assistant. What's keeping you from going back to school and changing careers? If finances keep you locked in your boxx, check into refinancing your house and taking out a loan to cover your education. Or are the real issues of school and homework more than you are willing to attempt? Are those the *real* issues holding you back?

Perhaps you've been in real estate for years but work-

The Treadmill Boxxes

ing evenings and weekends keeps you from spending the time with your family. You have a passion for computer graphics and design. Perhaps you could design websites from home. What would it take for you to make that jump? What are you willing to risk?

Or maybe you've been in management and would just love to punch a time clock for a change and leave all the managerial headaches to someone else. What's stopping you from stepping off your treadmill and trying something else? If it turns out that you hate the new job, just try another!

People from my parents' generation worked 30 or 40 years at the same job. In part, longevity was revered by both employees and employers. Yet, were these people happy all those years, or did they stay just because that's just what people did then? In today's economy, most companies can't promise the same job security that my parents enjoyed. Layoffs happen every day. So don't feel like you owe your employer your life! Remember to take care of *you* first – especially as it pertains to your career. Its uncomfortable side effects will certainly spill over into your relationships and health if you don't.

Yes, these are challenging times, but if you want something badly enough, you will find a way. It may mean that you have to move to another part of the country, or take a reduction in pay. It may mean that you have to go back to school. It may mean that your kids have to help out more at home. Yet, if you really want to make a change, the only thing stopping you is YOU. It may not be an immediate change. You may need to think about each step involved and put a plan together to get to your destination. But it is still your choice and making the decision to begin taking whatever steps are necessary is the first step.

Many of us decided what we wanted to be when we were 18 years old. At the time I was ready to go off to college, the majority of women became secretaries, teachers, or nurses.

Get Out of Your Boxx

What I wanted most at that time was to be a physical education teacher; however, there was a glut of teachers then, so I decided to look elsewhere. As it turned out, my mother was hospitalized when I was in high school and that experience opened my eyes to the world of nursing. One of the things I hated most was not understanding the information that the doctors and nurses shared with me about her condition. That drove me to learn more. So, between my curiosity and the trend at the time, the logical direction for me was nursing.

I enjoyed nursing for a long time until my position in management quickly educated me about the term "nursing burnout." However, that basic education, including a master's degree in the field, led me in other paths from there. I ended up in medical sales for several years, where my nursing background gave me certain advantages in selling to nurses. My education and first career helped me in my ability to deal with people, develop intuition, and demonstrate strong skills in written and verbal communication, organization, public speaking, and time management — skills that apply to a variety of situations and careers.

Did I ever dream that I would become a motivational speaker, or that I would make a great deal of money in medical sales, or that I would sell advertising for a newspaper, or be a columnist and write a book? Heavens, no! I just thought I would be a nurse my whole life like so many of those women who put in their 40 years and then retired! I guess I've been thinking "Out of the Boxx" for a long time and just didn't know it. If I got bored with a job or didn't find it fulfilling, I found another one. The people I have met along the way have taught me many things. The possibilities I discovered by keeping my eyes and my mind open to change were incredible. Looking back, I am so glad that I didn't just stay in nursing, although I have no regrets taking that path originally. I relish many of the memories. Yet, had I realized the many other possibilities available to me at age 18, I may have chosen a dif-

The Treadmill Boxxes

ferent route entirely. I think I would have enjoyed television broadcasting or perhaps advertising. But how could I know about those possibilities living in small-town America in 1974? I didn't. I started with a traditional female role and reshaped it for myself as I went along.

I invite you to do the same. Examine the Career Boxx you live in and see if it's working for you, or is it holding you back in some way? Do you want to wake up excited about life, or are you satisfied with the status quo? All I can tell you is that the zest for life I have found in writing this book has been keeping me up until 3 a.m. because I am so excited about what I am doing! I only seem to need about six hours of sleep a night now. That tells me I am on the right track. Compare that to my life prior to my Mexican journey when I was requiring 10 or 12 hours of sleep a night, simply due to depression and feeling unfulfilled. I love typing like crazy into the wee hours of the night wondering where my mind and this book will go next! The power, the energy, the passion are all flowing like crazy in me and it's wonderful!

It can be the same for you, if you find your passion. Don't let the Boxx of the Wrong Career keep you on the hamster wheel. Get off and see what else life has to offer. It's up to you. Just decide.

"So long as you have the power to choose, you have the power to change."
Dr. Phil McGraw

Chapter 9
A Weighty Boxx

The Weighty Boxx has many sides: From mildly overweight to obese, anorexic or bulimic, or even compulsive bodybuilding. But what do all these things have in common? They are all tied to body image – both the inner as well as the outer image, reflected to ourselves as well as others. What you see in the mirror is not necessarily what others see, or even what your brain sees and accepts as true. Personal perception and lifelong beliefs of love and acceptance, combined with values of our society and family, help to shape the Weighty Boxx for each of us. Add to that the media's incessant portrayal of the "perfect body"— one appearing completely starved — it's no wonder that the path to self-esteem and confidence becomes confusing for many. Whichever side of the weight issue you fall on, the Weighty Boxx is an emotionally heavy burden to bear if you're held captive by it. Over seven million women and one million men battle eating disorders in the United States alone, yet it is not the weight (or lack of) that is the key – it is the underlying issues that are truly important.[iii]

Have you fought your weight for years? Either too heavy or too thin? Or maybe you don't think you're too thin, but others constantly tell you that you are. Or are you a perfectionistic body builder, sculpting to the point that everything else in your life is secondary? Then perhaps you are living in the Weighty Boxx.

A Weighty Boxx

Let me clarify that when I mention body builders, I am not criticizing people who take care of their bodies, whether through body building or any other form of exercise. If more of us took time to regularly work out and eat right, many of our health problems such as heart disease, diabetes, and stroke would be non-existent. What I am saying is that any of these behaviors, taken to the extreme, can put both your emotional and/or physical health in danger. That is when the boxx itself has stopped being useful and has become dangerous.

Whether you are overweight or underweight, your self-esteem may be in constant turmoil. It affects your feelings of how you are accepted as a person, employee, spouse, friend, parent, or any other role you fill. Living in the Weighty Boxx may limit your opportunities at the same time it adds stress. For example, a runway model's career dictates that she must be ridiculously thin to keep her job. In relationships, spouses or significant others may worry about your weight and how it affects your health, or may criticize you for it, adding to your stress. Physical conditions like chronic fatigue or joint problems can take their toll on the body, as knees and hips take on extra strain when carrying an overweight body. For the anorexic or bulimic, other health issues such as malnutrition and loss of bone density may result due to insufficient vitamins and minerals in the diet.

Perhaps the worst part is the emotional drain from being held captive in these boxxes. Feelings of low self-worth, self-loathing, depression, anger, sadness, hopelessness, lack of energy, absence of joy when looking towards the future, and so many others, leave victims so deeply stuck that they find it hard to ever see the light of day. As a result, many fight these battles unsuccessfully all of their lives.

Again, you must decide if this boxx is working for or against you. That protective Body Armor Boxx applies here as well. Maintaining an ideal weight is healthy. If you consider centuries past when people spent most of their waking hours in search of food, those who had a little extra "padding" fared best, since finding and killing the next meal may have taken a few days! Although we don't have those issues today, a few extra pounds may act as a safety net in case sudden illness attacks the body. An underweight person is at a distinct disadvantage during a severe bout of flu as the weight lost during this illness could seriously delay recovery.

On the other hand, keeping your weight so that it doesn't get out of control is extremely beneficial. If you tend to gain weight easily, you may want to give yourself a bit of room and keep your weight a few pounds under your ideal goal for breathing room during the holidays or other times when overeating is most common. Either way, only you can decide if the Weighty Boxx is holding you captive or keeping you safe. If captive, think about why you are held there and then make a choice to stay or escape, but remember that the road to discovery involves more than taking a diet pill. This boxx, as with all the others, must be studied on a deeper level to understand the true issues involved.

The Overweight Boxx

Our nation is known for so many big things — the Super Big Gulp, big houses, big screen TVs, and sadly, — a lot of big people. Obesity has risen to new highs. Our lifestyle over the years, changing from that of hunter-gatherers to that of sedentary computer workers, has done us no favors when it comes to our health and physique. Remote controls, drive-up windows, and numerous other "conveniences" have limited our caloric usage even further. Add to that the daily stress we carry, and it's no wonder we are addicted to a variety of "coping" mechanisms, from tobacco, to alcohol, to drugs, and yes, to food. It is the "socially acceptable addiction" for any age group. Whether you have been carrying ten extra pounds that have been driving you nuts for years, or you are clinically obese, the underlying cause and effects can be the same. While the obese person may wonder why her friend worries about carrying ten extra pounds, those ten pounds can be just as emotionally weighty and burdensome to the thin person as the 50 or more are to the obese one. The inner issues driving them both may be identical.

The Opposite Extreme

Opposite of the overweight person are those people who never feel thin enough or beautiful enough. Anorexics (who practically starve themselves and work out compulsively, lest they gain a pound), or bulimics (who binge on junk food and then force themselves to vomit to purge their guilt-ridden minds of the empty calories) are both striving to achieve the perfect bodies. Body builders or those who compulsively exercise may fall into the same belief system.

Randy

Randy, a friend of mine whom I hadn't seen in years, looked terrifyingly underweight on one of my visits to see him. I was shocked by his appearance when he met me at his front door, wearing only his gym shorts. Each rib protruded distinctly, as did his "xiphoid process," a very small bone at the bottom of the breast bone. About the size of the last joint of your little finger, it is rarely visible in people of normal weight, but as it stared back at me, I caught my breath in concern. His weight was dangerously low. As I carefully approached the subject and asked him how much he weighed, he admitted that he didn't weigh himself — that a scale was just another way people judged themselves and each other. That was a red flag to me. I recognized that he was battling an inaccurate self-image. As we talked about it, he mentioned that when he was a child, he was "chubby." As a result, he was always the last to be chosen to be on any sports team. That emotional scar led him to believe that his personal value was tied to his physical appearance. Thus, terrified of ever falling to that depth of despair again, he had made it a life-long commitment to never allow himself to get overweight. As a result, he had evolved into an "exercise machine" whose regimen never varied, and he had sculpted himself a body that was nothing but rock hard, lean muscle stretched over bone. What he couldn't see was how desperately thin he had become and how dangerous that might prove to be in the long run.

How Do They Change?

How do people finally reach a point where they are determined to shed the excess weight or stop a self-destructive eating cycle? How do they find some inner direction to do so? Even more importantly, why are some people successful where others are not?

I believe it all comes down to understanding the deeper issues that hold us to our weight. The conscious and the subconscious minds are two entities that quite often have very different messages. Lifelong subconscious beliefs can have very strong influences on the conscious mind, and until the two can work in harmony, one will always win out —usually the subconscious.

For example, you can make a conscious decision to lose ten pounds to look better, feel better, fit into your clothes more comfortably, or to look good for your upcoming high school reunion. However, if your subconscious has other ideas, no diet or weight loss plan will ever work, no matter how hard you try. Those negative voices that chase around in your head can defeat you before you ever get started. Have you ever heard anyone say, "I sure hope this diet works. The last ten I've tried surely didn't!" This person's subconscious has already convinced her that this diet won't work either. Why? Because some life-long, unconscious message is the one truly making the decision, and until she can identify that message she cannot change it.

It can be a complicated road to discover what is really at the root of your unconscious beliefs about your weight. Childhood issues of acceptance, as well as beliefs of not being good enough, smart enough, and/or pretty enough can come into play, just to name a few. Being teased at school for being too fat or too thin can cement life-long beliefs that you will always be that way. Or in Randy's case, his pain of being called "chubby" was so overwhelming that he became driven by fear and has literally been running ever since.

For me, I think it started in high school. I was never one of the popular kids. I used food to cope with stress and became a "sweets junkie." I ate to feel better. Or perhaps not to feel the hurts that surrounded being a kid in a sometimes unfriendly world. I have struggled with that pattern for years. Fortunately, my love of athletics and being outdoors always helped me to balance my caloric intake, or my weight could have easily gotten out of hand. Typically, when I reach a point that my jeans get uncomfortable, I put my foot down and stop my bad eating habits, and bring my weight back in line simply because I refuse to buy larger clothes. Although I am more comfortable and happier with myself when I weigh ten pounds less than normal, I am not driven to lose those last ten pounds. Yet, I always keep "wishing" that I were that ideal weight. The problem is that I am not willing to put in the consistent work to get my weight there, much less maintain it there. So I settle for feeling "acceptable and good enough" right where I am. The point is that I need to be more honest with myself and just admit that I really don't mind weighing ten pounds extra. Then I don't have to beat myself up every time I get on the scale and discover those ten pounds are still there!

Despite being able to maintain my weight within ten pounds of my goal, I still use food as a source of comfort, especially during times of stress. I can justify eating an entire box of Girl Scout Thin Mints in a ten-minute sitting, which is definitely NOT healthy! Food comforts me in low times and rewards me in good times. Fortunately, although I may not be motivated to lose my ten pounds, I do recognize that eating hundreds of calories of sugar and chocolate is not a behavior I am proud of, nor does it help my body in any way. Thus, I have made a conscious decision to do a better job of balancing my wants with my needs, and am constantly working towards that goal to achieve better overall health. I can't say that I have permanently won the battle, but I can say that I have an exceptional awareness of it, and as a result I have begun to break down the walls of my boxx, little by little.

Whatever your deeper issues may be, they are probably at the root of what is inhibiting your weight loss. Until you can locate and identify your real self-conflicts, the work you do towards diet and/or exercise may be extremely hard to follow and may lead you, once again, to failure.

How do you discover and face these issues? Think Outside the Boxx! A psychotherapist may be able to help you unravel the secrets. Perhaps hypnosis or other alternative methods can open up channels you haven't yet reached. Journaling about your feelings may bring up additional issues that you have buried. Then you need to decide if you want to accept those past beliefs for the rest of your life, or if it's high time you change them. Sounds easy, but it will take some work. Lifelong patterns do not change overnight.

It might take a life crisis to win your life-long battle over your subconscious and convince yourself that change is possible. You may have already realized exactly what your deeper issues are, but you're still not motivated to change. Then, a monumental event occurs, giving you a reason to get serious about the issue. A brush with death may suddenly cause a shift in perception. If you were diagnosed with diabetes and knew that you faced daily insulin shots if you didn't suddenly lose 30 pounds, might that strike enough fear in your

A Weighty Boxx

soul to make you initiate a new lifestyle? A sudden heart attack may become the driving force for you. Realizing that your three young children still need you to take care of them may be the impetus to changing your eating habits.

A promise to a loved one may carry enough power to help you take that first step. Al Roker, from the *Today Show*, fought obesity all his life, and finally found his inner strength to take serious some steps after promising his dying father that he would lose weight.

If you really want to lose (or gain) weight, first ask yourself why? If you could wave a magic wand and the weight disappeared, how would your life be different? Perhaps leaving the heavy you behind and moving on to a thin you holds more fears than perceived benefits.

Jackie

A woman named Jackie unknowingly revealed to me her own unconscious fear of weight loss success. She told me she'd love to lose 30 pounds and be more self-confident. So I asked her to close her eyes and to pretend that she had achieved both wishes. What did her life look and feel like then? After thinking about it for a few minutes she replied, "Yes, I can see the benefits, but what if my husband divorces me?" It took me a minute to realize she was dealing with the Boxx of Fear of Success. She wondered what would happen if she finally succeeded in her battle, lost the weight, and felt strong and confident, but in the end was no longer the person her husband had married 15 years earlier. What if he didn't like the new person his wife had become? What if he divorced her because she was different? I turned the question back to her and asked her what if he loved her even more? What if he was excited that she felt better about herself? What if their relationship went to the next level up, not the next level down? What if the possibilities she created with her new identity encouraged her to apply for a job she had always dreamed of?

Get Out of Your Boxx

What if that job allowed them more time off and an increased income as well? Why was she talking herself out of the things her conscious mind knew might be beneficial, and letting her very mixed-up unconscious mind run the show?

If we don't recognize the powerful role our subconscious plays, it will run our lives completely, whether we want it to or not.

Check in with your subconscious and ask yourself some deep questions about what really drives you before you start on the next fad diet that comes down the pike. For some people, weight is an unconscious protection from the outside world. It may even provide a certain unconscious belief of safety from unwanted sexual advances. Perhaps they were sexually abused when they were young and learned early on that by downplaying their sexuality through carrying extra weight, they felt that they prevented further trouble. A woman named Trudy told me that she had actually lost a lot of weight between high school and college. Although she was thrilled with her new, curvy self, her happiness was short-lived as she was raped during her freshman year in college. The lesson she learned? It's safer to be heavy.

Perhaps you wonder if your spouse truly loves you unconditionally and you unconsciously test the waters by gaining weight. Wendy confessed to me that her husband had told her when they married that the only reasons he would divorce her would be for infidelity or if she gained weight! What a huge burden she carried with that knowledge!

There is another end of this spectrum. There are those who struggle to keep their weights at excruciatingly low numbers, or who constantly overwork their bodies into submission, striving for the "perfect body." I challenge them to look around. How many truly "perfect" bodies do you see every day? Unless you compete in body building competitions, or are a waif-thin model surrounded by others of a similar look, the perfect bodies in this world are extremely rare indeed. Why do so many women strive to look like an unrealistic Barbie Doll when Barbie's proportions are not humanly possible to begin with? It is an illusion some will chase forever, and when it proves unattainable, they chastise themselves even further. Many years ago, the famous singer Karen Carpenter, died of anorexia in her ongoing battle to reach for the perfect figure. Fortunately, my very thin friend Randy began to make some changes. Although he still lives deeply entrenched in the Weighty Boxx, he has at least cut himself a window in his boxx to see daylight – he has gained about 15 pounds and actually gets on the scale from time to time. It's progress – one small step at a time.

On the other hand, if on your road of self-discovery you find out that you really *don't* want to gain or lose weight because you are completely satisfied with yourself just the way you are, then that's fine. Just remember – if you are in fact content with yourself, then it shouldn't matter what anyone else thinks. Be happy with who you have chosen to be! If the Weighty Boxx works for you and you can admit that losing (or gaining) weight is just not your priority and it DOES NOT impact your health, then admit it is your boxx and go on. Just don't use it as an excuse or allow yourself to be its victim. We all make choices, and just as with the others, you can chose to live in this boxx or break out of it. The choice is yours.

"The past does not equal the future."
    Anthony Robbins, motivational speaker

Chapter 10
The Unfulfilling Empty Boxx

*E*mptiness. That feeling that leaves you emotionally heavy, without energy, lost, directionless, or questioning your own value in life. What causes some people to find themselves in the Boxx of Emptiness? I'm not really sure, but I can tell you that I've been there and it's not at all pleasant. It seems horribly hard to climb out of, extremely difficult to understand, and it almost cost me my life.

I didn't always feel empty. I certainly wasn't born that way. Nor did I go to school or start my career or family with those feelings. I always had goals. First, to graduate from high school. Then college. Then to get my first job in nursing and make some reasonable money. Next, to buy a house and have a child. My lifelong passion, however, had always been to own my own horses. That desire, although in the background, always drove me steadily on. As I accomplished each goal I set for myself, the next one would always begin forming in my mind, if it hadn't already been there for years.

When my daughter was seven, we were able to buy a small ranch in the country. Finally, I got the horses I had always dreamed of owning since I was a child! (My parents had refused to buy me one as they were convinced my interest in horses would be short-lived. Little did they know it would be a life-long passion!) I was fortunate that my daughter shared my love of horses and we spent countless hours riding and competing together in our "labor of love." For several years we

The Unfulfilling, Empty Boxx

lived and breathed horses from morning until night, including getting up at 5 a.m. to attend horse shows throughout the region and sometimes beyond.

Yet, somehow, as the years went by, the Empty Boxx began to entrap me. The empty feelings started to become an ever-present, prevailing fog that effected each day of my life. I think it started to appear when I decided to stay home with my young daughter and leave my career on the sidelines for a few years. Although I had returned to work six weeks after she was born, and had needed to work full time for the next several years, there came a point when our financial situation was strong enough to allow me the flexibility of staying home. In addition, I had begun to realize that with both my husband and I working what seemed to be 60-hour weeks, and mine including a tremendous amount of travel as well, we were completely missing our daughter growing up. As it turned out, I was glad that the time I decided to stay home was when she was between 10 and 18 years old. While many mothers prefer to stay home when their children are babies, I was glad to discover that staying home when mine was in the pre-teen and teenage years seemed to provide her with a great sense of stability during what can be the most complicated and confusing time in a child's life. After all, how much peer pressure do babies face compared with that of a teenager being pulled in a variety of ways at a time when they feel immortal and all-knowing at the same time? Being home to set boundaries and to know exactly where she was and whom she was with, gave me a huge sense of relief. I knew I made the right choice.

I stayed incredibly busy during these years, despite not working outside the home. I volunteered hour upon hour with my daughter's equestrian group, organized events, served on national committees, answered a zillion phone calls, and just basically gave of myself, my time, and my energy. But somewhere along the line I began to feel the emptiness. It started out as something small and nebulous, but over time it grew like a tumor, taking over my body and my mind, piece by piece, until it left me terminally affected from the inside out. It was certainly not that I didn't enjoy being home, because I really did. I loved the time I was able to spend with my daughter — those are days that I will always be grateful for, especially since I realize that not all parents have that luxury. My bond with her is, in part, as strong as it is now because of all the time I was able to spend with her during those years.

Yet, what caused me to feel unfulfilled? At some point I finally realized that I hadn't found a new goal to work towards, and had not had one for a long time. My life revolved around everyone and everything else. In addition, I had always defined myself by my roles and not by who I really was. My value, when I had contributed to our family income, gave me a sense of worth. I could measure it in the dollars and cents I deposited from my paycheck each week. If we needed new carpeting for the house, I knew I helped contribute to the purchase through the money I earned through my work. I remember wanting a new wooden fence around our property and my husband saying to me, "Well, just go sell something," knowing that if it truly was my goal, that nothing would stop me. I only had to put my mind to it. As a commission sales person at the time, I had the ability to drive myself like crazy to accomplish any mission towards the purchase of the next family necessity! I was a workaholic extraordinaire!

Well, suddenly becoming a stay-at-home mom, leaving my career and paycheck behind, I started to believe that I no longer had any value. I was no longer an equal partner in our family finances. Sure, I did the grocery shopping, laundry, child care, made meals, drove the car pool, got my daughter to her riding lessons and horse shows, but there was no paycheck at the end of the week. Only my husband brought one home. In my eyes, it became very easy to put him on a pedestal as the "breadwinner." I no longer felt equal or important. I kept my days filled with activities that seemed relevant and significant

The Unfulfilling, Empty Boxx

in my daughter's development. Yet, they just never seemed like enough, not to me and, in *my perception,* not in the mind of my spouse either. He was much more comfortable judging things in dollars and cents. As a result, he had a much harder time putting a dollar value on what I did with my time, which left me feeling even less valuable. It became a constant tug-of-war to try to find value and a sense of worth as I struggled with the cultural beliefs of monetary gain versus motherhood as a profession. I fell headlong into the Unfulfilling Empty Boxx and I stayed there for years.

During those days I often remembered thinking about something I had learned in nursing school regarding longevity. Apparently, many people only live for a short time after they retire, perhaps because they believe their self-worth and personal identity are tied to their job, and that without that "role" they simply don't know who they are anymore. I understood that feeling so well. I kept attempting to stuff more and more activities into my day, but none of it filled the huge hole within me. I even spent time volunteering at a home for troubled boys, trailering my horse there every week to give lessons to one particular boy who was interested in learning how to ride a horse who could jump fences. While I developed a strong bond with him and felt as though I may have made a small difference in his life, what I realized later was that I wasn't volunteering to satisfy my own desire to help those in need; instead, I was really seeking recognition and validation from others. Unfortunately, the praise I did receive never felt like enough, and I still felt empty and unfulfilled.

I continually struggled to try to meet the expectations of others and worried about what they thought of me. This only further confused me, misleading me even more into believing that what I did, and who I was, held no value whatsoever. (See Chapter 15 regarding the Expectations of Others.) Fortunately, my passion for my horses and my daughter kept me functioning on a daily basis, but the inner voice which de-

Get Out of Your Boxx

fined me had still not surfaced, and kept me boxxed up more tightly than anyone ever knew.

What I didn't understand at that time was that my feelings of worth had to originate, and be discovered, within myself. No one else could give it to me. The only person I needed to convince that I was valuable was ME.

How can you combat this Boxx of Emptiness? I believe it must start with the discovery of *who you are*. This realization lives deep inside you, not on the outside. To gain a clearer understanding of this concept, imagine what life would be like if you were dropped on a desert island — without your family, your job, your cell phone, your possessions, or anything else you think "defines" you. Who would you be? What would be important to you? What would you do to fill your days? What would you think about? If all your needs for safety and food were met, and you could have one special thing of your choosing, (excluding TV, the Internet, or your family) what would it be? A computer so you could write your feelings, memoirs, and stories to leave as a legacy? Your dog because your innate bond with animals makes you feel understood and loved? A camera to record your experiences in paradise to share with the world? Or perhaps you'd spend your entire day gardening and pruning each and every plant on the island because you love making things grow and feel wonderfully satisfied being surrounded by Mother Nature?

As you ask yourself those questions you will start to uncover the real you – the person who lives deep inside under all those superficial roles you carry around. The role of parent, employee, spouse, housecleaner, chauffeur of the carpool, keeper of the finances, mower of the lawn, vacation planner, social director, and any and all the other roles you or someone else puts upon you. Seeking these answers can help you discover who you really are and, as such, begin finding your way out of the Unfulfilling Empty Boxx.

In the movie *Castaway*, Tom Hanks' character was a

The Unfulfilling, Empty Boxx

frantic, harried Federal Express employee who was stranded on a desert island. During the four years he waited to be rescued, he filled his time with memories of his girlfriend. She was his lifeline when he was empty beyond despair. At the same time, he developed survival skills, talked to himself a lot, and was utterly transformed by his experience. His time alone gave him the space to hear his inner voice reveal the things that were truly important to him. He found his own "meaning in life." When he finally returned to the civilized world, he discovered he was drawn in an entirely new direction, with a different appreciation of who he was and new possibilities of where he might go. The fast-paced world he used to live in no longer "defined" who he was, or how he chose to live. He had a new appreciation for the little things in life and a deeper understanding of what was truly important and what only *seemed* important. He discovered a new world of possibilities by surviving a horrific ordeal that, in the end, perhaps made him stronger. We are left with the sense that he had a new perspective about time and how he would use it differently in the future.

If you were stuck on a desert island without all your worldly possessions, your family or career, just exactly *who* would you be? If you only find emptiness in your life now, then you have lost (or perhaps never found) your clear direction. Your inner voice hasn't told you what is truly important, what inspires you, what your passion is.

Here's another way to study this question. Imagine for a moment that a magic wand has been waved over your life and you can have anything you want except you can't change your attachment to any of your blood relatives. (Sorry, you're stuck with them – although you can change your marital status.) You have won the 100 million dollar Superball Lottery and have all the money you will ever need at your fingertips. There is nothing holding you back – you can do or be anything you can possibly dream of. You can start a new business and know that even if it failed, you would have plenty of money to fall back on and could try a completely different business if the first one didn't work out. You could spend every day volunteering for your favorite charity. You could travel the world for the rest of your life. You could establish a ranch for homeless children and fill it with horses and buffalos and chickens and dogs and whatever else you wanted. You could become an actor, and if no one would hire you to act in their movie, you could finance and produce it yourself because money was no object. You could move to Cozumel and become a diving instructor and spend every day of your life experiencing the wonders of the sea. The possibilities are endless and as unique as you. So, what would you do?

I suspect that you would probably spend the first year doing a variety of things, but after your initial excitement died down and you'd gotten tired of traveling or sleeping all day, what would you really want to do to fill your day? What would motivate you to get out of bed every morning?

Start deciding what you *really* want to be in life. If you're a secretary but what really gives you excitement and joy is gardening, then it's no wonder you feel empty facing a computer at the office every day! If you wish you'd become a veterinarian instead of an engineer, and you're bored to tears each day you go to work, it's hard to pull yourself out of that Empty Boxx so you keep hitting the snooze alarm over and over again every morning. If you're dying to stay home with your kids but the need for a paycheck keeps you going out into the workforce every day but leaves you miserable, then it's time that you start thinking "Out of the Boxx" to find a way to make your life more meaningful and less empty. Remember, the possibilities are out there, if you know where and how to look for them. But if you're walled up in your boxx you will *never* discover them.

Find a way to stop the noise in your life and listen to that voice within you. You may have to be very, very quiet to

The Unfulfilling, Empty Boxx

hear it, but it's worth it. If I hadn't finally heard the voice within me, you wouldn't be reading this today!

Then, once you know your true direction, start making a plan to make it work. If you really want to stay home and be with your kids while bringing in a paycheck, be creative and examine all the possibilities. Can you open a daycare center in your home and get paid for being home with the kids? Can you be a "virtual secretary" and do contract computer work from home? Can you make a living by sewing for others? Or, can you and your spouse arrange some creative scheduling? A lot of nurses I know work second shift, from 3 p.m. to 11 p.m., which allows them to be home with their kids for most of the day and their husbands to be home with them in the evening, thus never leaving the children in daycare. The down side to this arrangement is that the husband and wife don't get much time together, but they are passionate about their children always having a parent at home during the formative years.

If you are a secretary and really have a passion for gardening, check into what type of jobs might be available at a nursery or floral shop. You might be surprised at what is possible if you just do some investigation. The pay may be less, but the flexibility might provide more opportunities for family vacations or other benefits.

If you're an engineer and wish you could be a veterinarian instead, study the issues surrounding going back to school. With your background in engineering, the educational requirements to get through vet school might not be as bad as you think, and your happiness in a job you enjoy may lead to a happier family life as well.

No matter how you got stuck in the Empty Boxx, you can get out, although I think this boxx is one of the hardest to identify and understand. Do your homework and ask yourself some of these questions to start you on your path of discovery:

- ❏ Do I enjoy my job or career?
- ❏ What am I passionate about in life, and am I doing it?
- ❏ Do I watch the clock every day, hoping time will go faster?
- ❏ Do I feel as though I am meeting everyone else's needs but not my own?
- ❏ Do I feel listless and without energy?
- ❏ What are my goals? (Do I even have any?)
- ❏ Do I keep wishing for a time in the future when things will be different somehow?
- ❏ Do I feel unimportant in what I do every day?
- ❏ Do I find meaning and value in my life?
- ❏ Do I hate getting out of bed every morning, or do I jump out of bed, excited about the day?
- ❏ When I am lying on my deathbed, what will I hope to have achieved in my life?

These questions may prompt you to uncover others in your quest for personal identity and passion. Sometimes they may seem too personal when you begin to study yourself, so apply them to a close friend or loved one with whom you can identify. It might help you to see the path more clearly to begin with. Looking in the mirror can sometimes be misleading, so it may be helpful to ask that friend to help you see your reflection.

Again, remember that the boxxes affect the three areas of your life: career, relationships, and your personal health and well-being. How is being stuck in the Empty Boxx affecting you? Are you doing a mediocre job at work because you hate your job? Are you short-tempered with your partner or kids because you are unhappy with yourself? And what is going on within your body as a result of your choices? Do you suffer from migraines, restless sleep, battle your weight, or experience stomach problems? These, and more, could all be a result

The Unfulfilling, Empty Boxx

of living in the Empty Boxx.

If you're stuck in your career for some reason, at least find passion and excitement in another avenue of your life. Find a hobby that allows you the self-expression you are seeking. Get an outlet outside of work that gives you fulfillment. Painting, writing, bicycling, volunteering for a youth organization you feel strongly about, or taking up a new sport like golf, might give you something to be passionate about. If you knew you were going to ride your horse every day for an hour after work, wouldn't that make getting out of bed every day more exciting? Wouldn't you have something to look forward to? If that's the way you need to find your passion, then so be it!

Remember as with all the boxxes, you are not stuck there for life unless you choose to be. It is all about choices. The escape may feel slow and difficult at first, but if you are determined, there is a way. My father used to say, "Where there's a will, there's a way!" He wasn't kidding!

"As soon as you trust yourself, you will know how to live."
        Johann Wolfgang Von Goethe

Chapter 11
The Sex Boxx –
The Good, The Bad, And The Ugly

"Even bad sex is better than no sex," my friend Carol confessed to me as we were lying on the beach in Cozumel, discussing the good, the bad, and the ugly aspects of sex.

I looked at her in amazement. I was dumbfounded. "Not in my opinion," I countered. I had images of a frantic Lorena Bobbitt running through my head. She obviously hadn't believed that even bad sex was better than having no sex, and had sliced her husband's penis off to prove it.

Carol's comment made me realize that a chapter about the Boxx of Sex was a necessary component of this book. If she truly believed that, I suspected many other women *and* men in this country believed the same thing, and I felt a need to share my two cents worth on the matter.

The great thing about women is that they will tell other women their deepest feelings on a variety of subjects, and sex is just one of them. I don't know how much and what kind of details men share with other men, but suffice it to say that women will share details that can make a good smut novel seem dry and boring. So I started talking to anyone who would tell me what they thought about sex. Again, this was not an official research survey with a scientific questionnaire handed out to a controlled number of people – it was just open conversation with those who wanted to be heard. My job was to spend a lot of time listening.

Women, of course, were the easiest audience, for as I already said, they will generally jump into a topic like this with both feet – whether or not they know you personally. I had to tread a little more carefully with men, for their openness and approach to the topic comes from an avenue more foreign to me. Yet, I still found some interesting men who wanted to be heard. No matter what your sexual orientation, the behaviors and feelings of each person in the relationship and how it relates to the Boxx of Sex is what is important.

I have not used the real names of the individuals whose stories follow, but their thoughts and feelings are as accurate as I can convey. I asked them to tell me what they *really* thought about sex. How it affected their lives. What they wanted from it, liked about it, hated about it, or were just plain indifferent to. The stories were as varied as the individuals themselves and my early assumption was right – the Boxx of Sex is indeed The Good, The Bad, and The Ugly. Some people couldn't get enough of it while others hoped they'd never have to "perform" again.

Sex: A Bed Of Understanding Or A Position Of Power?

Most creatures on this planet have sex for the simple purpose of reproduction. Mother Nature calls males and females together for an annual sporting event of mating that sometimes involves males battling for females in a fight-to-the-finish dance. Yet, after all the fuss is over, both sexes go back to their busy lives doing whatever they do best, and for the lucky, offspring are a later result.

For human beings, however, sex is much more complex. We don't just have sex for reproduction, although that certainly comes into play. We have sex for so much more — for recreation, for pleasure, for feeling loved and secure, for discovering a connection to another person that just cannot be uncovered in any other way. We have intimacy. I don't just mean intimacy, as in the act of sex itself. I mean intimacy the way Dr. Phil McGraw recently described it: "Intimacy means trusting people enough to give them the power to hurt you." And that's where things get complicated.

Sure, there's sex just for sex. There's prostitution, or one-night stands, or any variation thereof, but that is purely the act of sex. There is nothing personal about it – not the intimacy involving trust. But what happens when two people come together sexually within the confines of a relationship? What do they want out of it? What seems to change for some couples between the time they begin dating and as the years go by? Do they continue to enjoy sex throughout their relationships, or does something occur that changes what was once wonderful into something routine, boring, or even unappealing? What happened to Lorena Bobbitt? I'm sure we'll never know the deep feelings that drove her to commit assault on her husband, but it is pretty apparent that sex for her was not a *Bed of Understanding*.

Sex has been used as a form of power for centuries, evidenced by rape throughout the course of history. Does rape really happen between a married couple, or does the marriage license mandate that sex is a given under all circumstances? Or if it is not true physical rape, are there other pressures put upon one or another in a relationship whereby one feels pressured into submission by the other, perhaps psychologically as opposed to physically? What happens in courtship to set them up to succeed or fail as their sexual relationship develops?

In less sexually open times in our history, many women married while they were still virgins. Their wedding night was the first time they actually had sex with their partner. For better or for worse, what they had was what they got. Whether their partner was good in bed or bad, loving or aggressive, that was who they had chosen to marry, and generally that was their destiny – at least, until such time that divorce or death would split them up. For some, since this was their only knowledge of sex, that may have been acceptable, as they would have no basis of comparison upon which to judge their situation.

In today's more promiscuous society however, the number of people who remain virgins until their wedding night is significantly lower than in earlier years. While I am not here to debate whether this is morally right or wrong, I do believe that it provides individuals with a broader knowledge base concerning what they do and don't like in a sexual partner. Hopefully, they can then choose a partner who is more compatible to their own personal preferences. In other words, a woman who marries and first experiences sex on her wedding night may be completely overwhelmed with a very aggressive lover for a husband which may leave her fearful of sex throughout her life. Yet, that same woman, had she been more experienced and selective, may have found a partner who was more reserved and compassionate, yielding a lifetime of more satisfying lovemaking.

"At least bad sex is better than no sex?"

I don't think so.

Sex can be the most wonderful act that can bring two people together, but when it's not, it can be a *Position of Power and Control*, or it can be a *Weapon that Wounds*. If you are Boxxed in by Sex, *do something about it!!* Just like the other boxxes, it will affect your effectiveness in your career, the way you feel about your relationship, and even overlap into your health – either emotional or physical. Issues of self-esteem are closely tied to your feelings about sex, and if your self-esteem is shaky, odds are everything else will be too.

Remember the Body Armor Boxx exists within this boxx as well. When beginning a relationship with a new sexual partner, that boxx can help you to set boundaries and establish

Get Out of Your Boxx

behaviors that are "off limits," leaving you more comfortable to begin to build a relationship based on trust. By educating your partner about what behaviors you enjoy and those that you don't feel comfortable with, you begin to build the *Bed of Understanding* on which your enjoyment can grow. Yet, by not sticking up for yourself and your needs at the beginning, you start down the road of giving the other person in the relationship a *Position of Power* from which it becomes difficult to extricate yourself later.

As with all the boxxes, recognition is the key. Ask yourself some serious questions about your sexual relationship to determine if your boxx is working for or against you. These questions are a place to begin your investigation. You may think of your own questions from the list below. Again, if it is hard to look at your own life and recognize your behaviors and how they make you feel, start by examining a close friend's situation. Ask yourself these questions about a trusted friend who may have shared their details with you. It may help you first recognize issues in your friend's life, which you can then apply to your own.

- ❏ Do I enjoy sex with my partner?
- ❏ Do I feel safe telling my partner everything about how I feel regarding our sexual intimacy?
- ❏ Has the act of lovemaking changed dramatically over our time together – for better or worse?
- ❏ How often do each of us desire to have sex, and are we understanding and able to compromise with each other's needs for frequency?
- ❏ Does my partner understand if I am not in the mood for sex, or does he or she feel hurt, frustrated, or angry with me if I am not always a willing partner? Or do I get frustrated for this same reasons with my partner?
- ❏ Does my partner enjoy giving me pleasure as much

as he or she enjoys receiving it, and do I enjoy giving my partner pleasure as much as I enjoy receiving it?
- ❏ Do I feel in any way pressured to "perform" while having sex?
- ❏ Do I look forward to having sex, or does it make me feel anxious, threatened, or worried in any way?
- ❏ Can my partner and I enjoy physical closeness without it necessarily culminating in sex?
- ❏ Does my partner satisfy my overall need for sexual fulfillment?
- ❏ Does my partner respect my boundaries and not pressure me to do things that are uncomfortable for me, and do I respect his or her boundaries as well?
- ❏ Do either of us "keep score" as to how often we have sex?
- ❏ Is there ever anything painful involved, physically or emotionally?
- ❏ Am I unhappy with my sexual relationship and, if so, why? What can I do to change it?
- ❏ If I can do nothing to make the situation better, am I sacrificing myself in order to make my partner happy? If so, why am I not taking care of *me* first?
- ❏ What does sex mean to me?

These questions should get you started examining your own personal sexual situation. You may need to think about and journal your answers to these questions, and create other questions from there that can help give you the answers you need. The following stories describe how some individuals felt about their sexual experiences. Perhaps they will trigger some thoughts for you as well. Some of these stories are wonderful and some are horribly sad. As you will see, the Boxx of Sex can be different for everybody, yet one common theme runs true — it doesn't have to be bad and if it is, YOU DO have

Get Out of Your Boxx

the power to change it.

Their Stories

Jane

Jane is almost 60 years old and is in her second marriage. She first married right out of high school and thought that having a home of her own would be happier than living with her parents. What she soon realized was that she just acquired a new set of problems. While she loved her new found freedom from Mom and Dad, she discovered that her husband was definitely a believer in power and control. He had been raised in a family where the father and husband was "Master of the Universe," where everyone and everything revolved around his needs – including behaviors within the bedroom. Although Jane stayed married to this man for a number of years, raised a family, and carried on with her everyday life, she gradually built up a wall of anger and rebellion until she had to escape before her self-esteem was completely shattered. She relates two stories of sex which touched my heart and proved my point that even *bad sex is NOT better than no sex.*

Like many women, Jane enjoyed the intimacy of simply being held close with bodies touching. One of the behaviors she found especially satisfying was "playing spoons," where both parties would curl up like two spoons laying in a drawer – one facing away from the other, while the partner curled up to the first person's back. To her, this was a safe and comforting position which brought an incomparable closeness between her and her spouse. Yet, Jane's husband, Jack, refused to accommodate her desires. He felt she was turning her back on him and rejecting him. He would say to her, "I feel rejected when you lay like that. Don't do it," and he totally forbid the behavior. If Jack had only understood or cared that Jane's need for this closeness only added to her feeling of intimacy, it would have been a plus to their relationship. Instead, he put his feelings and needs first, as his own low self-esteem couldn't handle anyone else's feelings but his own.

For Jane, the intimacy itself was soon replaced by pure sex and nothing more. At first she tried to wean her husband from his frequency demands by the usual method: she complained of headaches regularly. At some point, Jack determined that he would give her adequate "space" by demanding sex *only* every other night. It didn't take Jane long to realize that once again, Jack was clearly demonstrating that his needs were more important than her own, as every other night was still too often for her and no other compromise seemed to be discussed. As the every other night program continued, Jane's anxiety and frustration reached its limit. One night, in sheer desperation, she rolled over onto her back with arms outstretched and proclaimed, "Go ahead. Just rape me and get it over with." It was not long after that incident that Jane left the relationship, realizing she had spent enough time not taking care of herself.

Fortunately, in her second marriage, she found a man who was more caring and sensitive and whose shy, quiet behavior gave Jane room to feel like she was an equal. Lovemaking became a sharing between two people, without pressure or performance expectations. Suddenly, the woman who didn't enjoy sex was seeing life from a totally different perspective. She got out of the Ugly Boxx of Sex, improving not only her self-esteem but her pure enjoyment of life and her relationship at the same time. She whole heartedly confirms that *bad sex is NOT better than no sex.*

Tye

Tye and Susan married very young and for all the wrong reasons. Each was lonely and had dealt with some sort of life crisis. After Susan became pregnant they were happy to start a family. Yet, since they had never really been in love but had only enjoyed companionship and the adrenaline rush of young sex, their commitment to each other was shallow at best. After several years and two kids later, Tye discovered Susan had been having an affair. His world was shattered. He left the relationship for an extended time, but eventually Susan convinced him to reunite for the benefit of their children. And so he did; however, the trust between them lay shattered forever, affecting every aspect of their relationship, especially sex. Lovemaking became a physical release and nothing else. There was no intimacy, no frequency, no experimentation, no joy, and certainly, no trust. Eventually the couple parted ways.

To his great happiness, Tye and a woman named Chelsea found each other. She too had lived through an unhappy marriage and they both understood what it felt like to be emotionally battered and bruised. At first, they were frightened and hesitant to trust each other completely, and yet they somehow found a way of taking special care to hold each other's hearts as if they were small, wounded birds, cradled softly in each other's hands. One thing they had learned from their earlier experiences was to set boundaries for their expectations of each other. When it came to sex, they were explicit as to what things they would and would not do, as well as what things they particularly enjoyed. Since Chelsea had felt pressured to perform oral sex upon her husband throughout the course of their marriage, that particular act left her paralyzed with fear. As Tye's true interest was to love Chelsea as a long-term partner, he respected her discomfort with this act and never asked her for it. He comforted her in the *Bed of Understanding*. Eventually, when she felt safe that he would never demand this from her, she began to initiate it on her own, as another way in which she could show him that she loved him and wanted to do everything to give him pleasure. Her fear of sexual pressure was replaced with sexual enjoyment.

Tye's fear of abandonment slowly gave way to trust, and he began to believe that Chelsea truly loved him for who he was. As their trust and intimacy grew, their lovemaking became a wonderful act of sharing which bound them emotionally closer together. They both found a way out of a bad situation and into a good one — by getting out of their previously confining boxxes.

Jillian

Jillian's inability to have an orgasm through the act of intercourse left her completely nervous about having sex. Although she was extremely orgasmic with masturbation and enjoyed the physical closeness that intercourse provided, she was hesitant to admit to her partner that she was unable to climax through intercourse alone. Thus, she fell into the self-destructive behavior of "faking" orgasms. In talking with her friends, she discovered that many of them might fake an orgasm occasionally, but she could not find one person who did it with regularity the way she did – leaving her feeling all the more "abnormal" in her sexuality. She tried various partners, attempting to find true intimacy somewhere, yet the reason she couldn't find it was that she was not willing to trust herself to be honest with her partner about her needs. She was deeply entrenched in the Boxx of Bad Sex, and it was proving to be unfulfilling and empty, at best.

In her continued search she ended up in a relationship with a man named Steve. An unusually sensitive man, Steve recognized that she was not being honest about her orgasms and brought it to her attention. At first, she tried to deny the behavior, but because his approach was not condemning or accusatory, she took a chance and risked explaining her physical needs to him. When she realized that he was not "disappointed" in her for not coming at the same time that he did during intercourse, but that he actually loved to help her orgasm through touch and exploration, her ability to truly be intimate began to take shape.

It took her some time to help Steve understand that the

pleasure she received during intercourse itself was incredibly fulfilling, even without orgasm. (It may be an assumption for some men that the orgasm itself is the end-all for women, when, in fact, this may not be true for every woman. For some, the pure physical closeness is perhaps a stronger satisfaction than even the need for the climax itself.) When Jillian and Steve began to give and receive the things they each needed for lovemaking to be most pleasurable, the relationship evolved into something much deeper than either had ever experienced. Jillian actually became multi-orgasmic, an event that she never anticipated. The love and trust in combination with sex is what made their relationship grow. Sex, for Jillian, became a beautiful act as compared to one that had previously left her feeling embarrassed, hesitant, and like a complete failure.

Jason

Jason was proud of being sensitive to the needs of women and pleased with himself that the few women he had been intimate with had always confirmed he was an excellent lover. He took special care to pay attention to every detail of what his partner desired, and then fulfilled that need – literally finding more joy in meeting his partner's needs, first and foremost, than his own needs. His excitement and satisfaction came from the realization that he made them happy. He took extra time to ask them carefully worded questions to discover what they liked, and then proved patient beyond words in his kind and slow delivery of their pleasure.

As Jason searched for a meaningful, long-term relationship, he wanted more than just a great sex partner — he wanted a great friend as well. So he took his time finding just the right person with whom he could share his life. As I spoke to him one day, he told me that he had found the most wonderful woman. She was beautiful, funny, intelligent, and a great companion. He was supremely excited – except for one thing.

He was highly concerned that she was completely non-orgasmic. As he went on to explain, Lexi had been in a bad marriage with a man who had used sex as a *Position of Power*, leaving her with the belief that sex had nothing to do with having her own needs met whatsoever. She had been fearful of sex for years, lest she not "perform adequately" to meet her husband's needs, and have him blame her for her failure. As a result, her fear and apprehension in the bedroom had left her unable to relax enough to be able to climax. These years of bad sex had left a lasting impression upon her and even though she was beginning to feel safe with Jason and to trust him with her body, she had still been unable to have an orgasm except through her own masturbation in private. The idea of doing so in front of a partner seemed impossible.

As Jason told me about the situation, I could see that he was genuinely upset. As I inquired further, I learned that his first concern was that he simply didn't understand how anyone could not achieve orgasm. In the back of his mind he was mildly concerned that she was lying about this piece of the complicated puzzle. Secondly, he was upset with himself for not being able to break down her walls and *give* her an orgasm. It left him feeling inadequate and like a complete failure. Lastly, he couldn't understand why she even had an interest in lovemaking if the end result was that she was unable to orgasm. He was considering leaving the relationship over this issue despite their otherwise incredible compatibility.

As I listened to him struggle with his feelings, I was glad that I knew him well enough to share a woman's perspective with him. I explained that if Lexi had been in a marriage that had left her feeling that sex was a *Position of Power*, it was no wonder she had the reactions she did. It did not mean she was abnormal or "broken." In addition, I explained how the act of making love for women can sometimes be totally about experiencing a physical closeness with another person, a closeness not attainable in any other way. Women thrive on being held, caressed, kissed, hugged and touched in a variety of ways. He could help her most by understanding that she was literally a "survivor" or her last relationship, and that through his kindness, support, and patience he was indeed providing her an environment in which to heal. He was also giving her other things she desperately needed — a healing touch, the permission to be herself, and hopefully, unconditional love. He was, in fact, helping her get out of the Boxx of Bad Sex. I explained how she might truly be in heaven during every moment he touched her, and that orgasm was not necessarily the driving force behind her need for intimacy. Finally, I reassured him that *he was not responsible* for "giving" her an orgasm – he did not need to put that pressure upon himself. It was important that he recognize his need to orgasm wasn't necessarily hers, and that was quite alright. As long as both parties were comfortable in getting their needs met and respecting the needs and boundaries of the other, the act of making love could become so much more than just sex. Exploration and discovery of sexual pleasure through differing methods could actually lead to new levels of satisfaction, and could prove to be the most exciting part of the entire event.

 I also shared with him that he might indeed become Lexi's sexual savior. By continuing to provide a safe environment for her to be herself, perhaps she would reach a level of trust with him that would take her on a path of rediscovering the possibilities of attaining orgasm with a partner. What better satisfaction could he receive than that? Offering her loving acceptance, and perhaps freeing her from the chains and scars of her past, could be the greatest gift he could ever give her. With this new information, Jason continued his relationship with Lexi and indeed, her evolution gradually helped her find a path of sexual satisfaction she never knew existed. Thank God, Jason had been open-minded enough to think outside his earlier boxx of what his sexual responsibilities were, and to see what they might become.

When Sex Means Love

I also met two people who had come to the conclusion that sex meant love. Although they had different reasons to believe that, the end result was still the same – they were both left unsatisfied in their search for love.

Kathy

Kathy received confusing messages about love throughout her childhood. Her father, a police officer in a small town, was revered by his community. He was "in charge" at all times. Kathy looked upon him with a belief that he was "all-knowing," and, as a result, worshipped the ground he walked on. She did anything to receive his love. What no one ever suspected was that he also molested his daughter regularly. Since these episodes started when Kathy was very small, she was unaware that her father's touching and fondling behaviors were not a normal show of affection. This pattern taught her that love only came with sexual behaviors as he was the strong, tough figure of a father at all other times. Although I don't know what role her mother played, it was obviously very minor compared to the towering figure of her father.

As a result of this early belief system, Kathy spends most of her adult life searching for a loving relationship, but ends up jumping from one lover to another in her never-ending quest for real love. She is quick to jump into having sex with men without stopping first to learn who they are on a more personal level. As a matter of fact, she proudly tells her friends that she'd rather have sex right away so that if it's bad she doesn't waste any more time on the relationship. She doesn't know how to establish intimacy involving trust as her childhood taught her not to trust others easily. She thinks that this position of holding back and not taking the more intimate, personal risks involved in trusting someone will keep her safe. Instead, it keeps her isolated in her Boxx of Bad Sex even though she has plenty of sexual opportunities to choose from. She has not learned that she needs to build her own self-confidence first, and then begin to take steps towards establishing real trust with a partner in order to find a more meaningful relationship. Until she can discover those other issues, she will probably continue on her road of unfulfilled love and disappointment.

Sam

Sam's story has different roots but results in a similar belief system. While Sam's family was not abusive in the typical sense, they were not great believers in showing outward affection. Regular doses of hugs and kisses and positive pats on the head were not offered. With five boys in the family, Sam's father kept their energy contained by teaching them proper behavior, strict manners, and to be respectful and God-fearing. Furthermore, he didn't want them to grow up to be "wimps," so whenever they skinned a knee or experienced some other childhood upset and came home crying, he ordered them to "Quit crying and be a man." Although Sam's parents loved their boys very much and thought they were giving them the necessary life tools, they didn't understand three very important things. First, children need and crave positive attention to develop into strong, self-confident adults. Second, they need a safe environment where it is OK to behave as a child and not a miniature adult. Third, they need to feel unconditional love no matter what. As a result Sam started to believe that love didn't really exist. It was only a myth depicted in the movies.

However, as Sam got old enough to become sexually active, he thought he finally found love in the act of having sex. The closeness, physical touch, words of affection, and pleasure of the orgasmic release led him to believe that "making love" was truly *being* loved. Having found this outlet, his sexual demands upon his wife for increasing frequency, led her to develop feelings of being overwhelmed and pressured. She started to recognize that if she didn't offer him sex on a frequent enough basis, he felt that she did not love him. She became convinced that he kept score as to how often they made love. After a while, the pressure she was under to "perform," led her to leave him as it was putting her in a Boxx of Bad Sex – for sex was no longer about two people sharing love and intimacy involving trust and mutual understanding. It was about Sam getting his need for love met in a manner that was unequal and demanding.

As you study the Boxx of Sex, take the time to look at the big picture as well as the details. It is my hope that some of these stories will help you see perspectives about your relationships, determine whether or not they are working, and from there you can make your choices about what to do next.

Remember, having *bad sex is definitely not better than having no sex* because bad sex can leave you with lifelong scars visible to no one but you. They can limit your ability to do your best and live life in a loving and intimate relationship. It is a choice you make between enjoying a sexual relationship that is a *Bed of Understanding* or one of a *Position of Power*. I know which one I'm choosing. Only you can make the choice for yourself. Whatever you decide let no one else make that choice for you.

"Intimacy means trusting people enough to give them the power to hurt you."
Dr. Phil McGraw

Chapter 12
Deadly, Secret Boxxes

Secrets. Remember the power they had over you, even as a child? Either someone had a secret they were keeping from you, in which case you had no power over the situation, or you had a secret and keeping it to yourself might have been one of the toughest things you ever had to do. Either way, over the long haul, being involved with a secret may have caused you a great deal of stress.

If your siblings intentionally kept a secret from you, you may have felt hurt, rejected, sad, devalued, or even disliked.

If a friend promised to keep *your* secret, you may have worried just how long he could keep it. You may have been afraid that he might let your secret out. The results of your secret being revealed to the wrong person may have given you sleepless nights, and taught you to understand the power of blackmail.

If you were given the task of keeping a secret, the weight may have been enormous – especially if the secret was something bad. It's one thing to keep a secret about what you and your siblings bought for your mom and dad for their anniversary, but it's quite another to hold onto something that you aren't sure you should keep secret to begin with. What if you knew who beat up your friend at school but you were afraid to tell because he might beat you up too? That is one very heavy burden to bear.

Deadly, Secret Boxxes

Then there are secrets we keep even from ourselves. Things we know, things we've done, or things others have done to us that we don't even want to tell ourselves.

What price do we pay for keeping such secrets? The variety of pain can be enormous: from anxiety to sleepless nights, restlessness, fear, depression, physical pain, emotional turmoil, unhappy relationships, dissatisfaction with your career, low self-esteem, defeatist behaviors, inability to keep friends, hostility, shyness, aggressive behavior, or overt withdrawal. These behaviors can all lead back to the Boxx of Deadly Secrets that, of course, leads back once again to the big Boxx of Fear.

There are many deep, dark secrets within our society: Issues surrounding abuse (physical, emotional, or sexual), breaking laws, cheating someone, misrepresentation, and a variety of others that can all lead to built-up anguish for the one keeping the secret, or hoping that someone else will not reveal one. Whatever the cause, the end result is clear — secrets can hurt profoundly. To compound the issue further, childhood secrets can be even more muddled and confusing. Decisions made by children who may not even understand the significance may look like completely different issues when those same children become adults.

For example, keeping the secret that your father touched you in inappropriate places when you were a child didn't seem so huge at the time it took place, but when you became an adult, the significance of those behaviors is something entirely different. Former Miss America, Marilyn Van Derber, was a testimony to that, having lived with her father's incestuous behavior for 13 years, and yet not recognizing the significance of that secret for decades. She only found relief from many of her physical and emotional issues when she gathered her courage and revealed her secret to the world. She found a way to be true to herself, even if it was years after the fact. Now she is an avid leader, educating others on how to stop abuse from happening, to recognize signs in victims, and to carefully support those who have lived through it. She is a hero to many for her voice gave many others the courage to find their own voice and take the first steps to their own recovery. You can read more about her story at www.MissAmericaByDay.com.

Childhood sexual abuse is perhaps the deepest, darkest Secret Boxx of all. The statistics are beyond imagination: one in three women and one in six men in the United States are victims of sexual abuse or assault before the age of 18. As a survivor myself, I was overwhelmed when I read those unbelievable numbers. Although my abusive encounters were short-lived, I felt as if surely I was the only one who possessed those terrible feelings. The only one who felt the anger, shame, and guilt that went along with the emotional scars those events had left upon me. The only one who kept asking, "Why me, God?" And the only one with this terrible secret I prayed would never get out.

Fortunately, I was one of the lucky ones. I did not suffer for years at the hand of a loved one. I did not end up with overwhelming fears that left me afraid to leave my own house, marry, or have children. I did not have chronic physical pain that left me unable to do the things I love. But these brief encounters left their scars on me, none the less.

For over 20 years I kept that deep, dark secret — even from myself. Literally. I had built such a wall around those horrible memories that it was as if I had sealed them up in a big box and put them high upon some closet shelf, hoping that I would never have to look at them again — until one day. I will always remember the exact moment that boxx literally fell out of the closet and hit me like a ton of bricks. Maybe not the date itself, but exactly what I was doing and when and where.

Let me explain. Victims of trauma, such as sexual abuse, often suffer from Post Traumatic Stress Syndrome. Just as soldiers who witness the terrible atrocities of war may have to bury those memories in some remote corner of their brains just to go on with life, victims of sexual abuse may do the same. Some veterans may have terrible memories come flooding back over them when they hear a car backfire, reminding them of the sounds of gunfire many years earlier.

Well, the case can be the same for survivors of sexual abuse. They may grow up, go to college, marry, and raise a family, never remembering that they experienced the abuse. Until one day something triggers a memory within them and the flood gates open, unleashing a deluge of emotions and feelings — and the victim's world comes to a screeching halt as they attempt to sort through reality, memories, confusion, fear and grief.

In other cases, survivors may be completely aware of the events that transpired. They may have told others about it, or preferred to remain silent. More than likely, they stayed silent. The overwhelming feelings of guilt experienced by these victims tends to lead many to keep their dark secret to themselves, lest anyone find out and discard them as dirty laundry.

Guilt seems to be a constant among survivors, despite the fact that the victim was not the perpetrator. Victims frequently feel that they held some responsibility for the events even though they were children at the time and the abusers were adults. Fear of being chastised for participation in the acts may carry more weight than the desire to tell someone and seek relief. In fact, some are blamed and some may not be believed. While some are believed, other factors may still leave additional pain and questions for the victim. For example, the speed which the events are "swept under the rug," or if the abuser gets punished with only a slap on the wrist, can leave the victim feeling devalued again. The risks of telling become obvious.

Complications arise when incest muddies the picture even further. How does a child tell a parent that the other parent or sibling is molesting them? Most young children do not even understand what molestation is and therefore, do not realize they are being taken advantage of — at least not until it's too late to get out. Many mothers, abused themselves by dominant husbands, are just as powerless to help their children fight back.

Recent publicity involving priests and their altar boy victims only reinforces just how secretive and seductive the most trusted members of our society can be. Priests, coaches, close family friends, and relatives can all leave scars upon children and not even be discovered for years, if at all. In addition, the sanctity of the priesthood clouds the issues even further and oftentimes makes all involved doubt the word of the child when accusing a "holy man." Although the overwhelming issues involving alter boys have stunned this nation, perhaps it has finally opened the eyes of many who were either unseeing or unbelieving, and at last the voices of the little ones are being heard. Unfortunately for some, not until many years after the fact.

Are you a secret survivor of childhood sexual abuse? With the statistics mentioned earlier, there are probably many people within your inner circle who are survivors, but would you guess it? Would you know them to look at them? Would you admit it to yourself if you were one of them? More importantly, do you realize carrying that secret pain for years and not doing something about it may actually be holding you back in some way? Maybe it affects your beliefs about your own personal value. Perhaps in how you relate to other people. Possibly in how you do or don't meet your goals in life. Or, unfortunately, in aspects of your physical or emotional health.

In my own case, I first relived these memories about 15 years ago, when something triggered it for me. I felt fear, guilt and anger. But above all, I felt shame. I only told my husband and my older sister about the events that had unfolded in my early adolescence. I didn't even tell my parents. I was too ashamed and guilt ridden, and was terrified that they wouldn't understand my pain – even 20 years after the fact. I saw a counselor for a few visits, but didn't really want to dwell on the issue once I uncovered it. The interesting result was that I actually buried all the memories once again — out of sight, out of mind. In a very short time, it was once again erased from my memory banks and since neither my husband nor my sister brought it up, it simply disappeared from my sight.

Then, 10 years later, another experience triggered the memories and this time it really rocked me. I brought it up to my husband and sister once again. They, of course, remembered the conversation I had had with them years before *but I did not! Believe it or not, I had erased the memories a second time! Totally and completely!*

Well, this time I decided to do something different. I decided to attack the matter head-on. First, I found a wonderful therapist. (As I look back on it, the one I had tried 10 years before was neither compassionate nor understanding — it's no wonder I didn't see her for very long.) I read every book known to mankind about sexual abuse. *The Courage to Heal* by Bass and Davis was my "Bible" as I read how other women shared many of the same experiences, feelings and behaviors that I had. I joined support groups specializing in adult survivors of childhood sexual abuse. The WINGS Foundation in the Denver area (www.wingsfound.org) was a great network of understanding women who were all in their own stages of healing, many of whom could not afford a traditional therapist and found this group their lifeline to survival. I started talking about it to anyone who would listen, and in the process of doing so, found others who had been secret victims as well. Once I opened my door to them, some of them began to think about opening theirs as well.

Then, I took the final steps in the process. First, I told my mother. (My father had already passed away.) My anticipation of this conversation was much worse than the actual event itself. We shared tears, grief, and love, but most importantly to me, she showed me acceptance, understanding, and unconditional love. It was the most important gift she could have given me.

Lastly, I confronted my abuser — one of the toughest but most powerful things I have ever done in my life. The amazing thing about this experience was that he admitted his guilt to me. I was shocked for I had anticipated his denial, and envisioned him accusing me of the wrongdoing. To the contrary, the guilt he had carried for so many years led him to purge himself, and his tears came in waves and sobs right along with mine. Although it is my personal choice not to associate with him further, I have learned to forgive him, which I have also come to realize was part of my road to recovery.

The healing was slow but cathartic and unbelievable. I felt the weight of a thousand stones lifted from my shoulders. In my mind, the feeling of guilt began to move from me to my abuser and eventually I was able to let go of the emotional power he had held over me. The signs of chronic depression began to subside and each day seemed filled with more sunshine than clouds. I started believing I was indeed, a valuable person. Victims of abuse often feel they have no value, for if they had truly been valuable, why didn't anyone save them?

That last feeling – *of finding my own value* – gave me a whole new direction within my life. I started to really believe that I deserved good things. That I could accomplish anything I put my mind to, that I didn't need others' approval to determine my self-worth, and that I could find happiness and contentedness within myself.

And so I bring my story to you with the hopes that it will help those of you who have kept your secret all these years to realize that perhaps it is time for you to heal too. Maybe now you will take that difficult, but freeing step of facing your past. Maybe just realizing that in any group of 100 women and men you might be with today, one third of them feel much like you do. You don't have to feel alone on this journey – there are many who understand. Many are traveling with you. Many can help you heal and move on to a new and stronger you. And you can help them as well.

I have spoken with so many women who were abused as children and I am amazed we are not as large as many national political groups. Actually, we are, but we are a silent group of survivors, believing our silence is keeping us safe when, in fact, for many of us, it is eating us alive. Much of the battle I waged about committing suicide was tied to my feelings of not feeling valuable, a direct result of the abuse. I spent years overachieving throughout my education and career, hoping no one would ever know what a "bad" person I was. My biggest fear was that if anyone ever found out, they would know how awful I was and they would reject me. I suffered from the big Boxx of Fear every day of my life, even if my memories were repressed. The Claustrophobia Boxx I lived in also kept me safe, yet added anxiety to my life. My relationship with my husband was clouded by fears I didn't even realize I had.

I have talked to women who remain locked in their Secret Boxxes and are still terrified to come out. Two had been abused by up to four perpetrators before they were 11 years old. One still fears leaving her house. She has considered suicide on many occasions but I suspect like me, the love of her small children holds her in survival mode. Yet the other woman overachieves in her attempt to help others. Her goal is to help people realize how much they matter, because in her own childhood, she felt she didn't. Through her work, she finds peace. Some have told me of their fear of men in general, sex in general, or even having children, as they fear what might happen to them.

This Secret Society doesn't even know about each other, for they are afraid to offer a tidbit to anyone – lest they be burned. I often throw little opening phrases out to women as the opportunity presents itself. I am amazed at how they immediately pour out their souls to me. I made a wonderful connection with a woman named Lea this year, when we were both at a meeting. We were sitting at the same table when another woman had stood to give away a door prize and announced that her success story that week was that her divorce from her abusive husband was finally over. I looked at Lea, sitting across the table from me, and could see something in her eyes that said she understood the pain. I simply commented to her, "Yep, I sure understand that," to which she replied, "Me too." As we stared at each other for a moment, we connected in such a way to know exactly what we were talking about, and within minutes had both confessed our childhood secrets to each other. She had rarely found anyone who would talk about the situation, and we have since shared many thoughts and memories, which has proven to be healing for both of us.

A woman named Lori told me that she had only twice ever risked telling two women in her family about how she had been molested by her father. Neither had believed her, and she had never brought up the subject again — her initial pain, now compounded by being devalued for a second time.

In another case, Gretchen confessed that her husband had been abused by a coach when he was a pre-teen. She hadn't known about it until many years into their marriage when he suddenly fell into a depression so deep that he wasn't even able to go to work. They nearly lost their house before she was able to discover the root of his pain and get him appropriate help.

Please know that you don't have to live your life like this. You *do* have the power to break out of this horribly lonely, confining boxx. Healing does come when you can let go of the secret. It is my hope that this book will help people start seeing the light at the end of the tunnel. It was even difficult for me to write this chapter, worrying about how my mother would handle "what other people would say" when the book was published. However, she has come to understand that she was neither guilty, nor could she have stopped this all too common occurrence. Young girls and boys have been molested for years, whether their parents were there to protect them or not. Our best cure for this painful situation is education, building self-confidence in our children, and teaching them (and ourselves as adults) to come forward and *not* to be afraid. If Miss America, who came from one of the wealthiest, most influential families in Denver, can be abused, then anybody can.

Whatever you do, don't suggest that someone who has been abused keep their deep, dark secret. By doing so, what you tell them is that they were indeed bad to begin with, or that they just didn't matter. They will feel even more ashamed as your words and feelings will only confirm their fears — that there is something wrong with them since they should have something to hide. And you reaffirm for them a *second* time that they have no value.

If you are a survivor, reassert your value. Believe in yourself. Take care of *you* first. Don't let the pain of some childhood secret affect you for the rest of your life. Fight back and win! Step outside your Secret Boxx and reclaim your life. Join those of us who have taken the first step – we will welcome you with understanding and tears of hope.

"Unless we go back, find the truth and confront the terror, our subconscious memories will run our lives, choose our relationships, dictate our career choices ... control us."
Marilyn Van Derber –

Former Miss America and incest survivor

Chapter 13
So Many Boxxes, So Little Time

There are so many, many boxxes that can trap us. Sometimes simultaneously. When I left on my Mexican adventure I was held captive by the following boxxes: I Can't, Depression, The Empty Boxx, My Past, Beliefs, Habits, Boredom, and Claustrophobia. They were all tied to my Fear of Failure, of the Unknown, of Not Being Loved, of Taking a Risk, of Looking Foolish, and so many more. There were probably others I didn't even recognize.

Thus far, I have given you an in-depth look at some of the more common and/or devastating boxxes I see people living in all the time. While I can't break the others down as thoroughly (or this book would be huge!) I do want to give brief comments on a few more and identify others that may play a part in your life. As you study them in depth, look at them under the microscope the way I dissected the other boxxes in the preceding chapters. Most of them have similarities. Remember to be honest and enlist the input of others whose opinions and values you trust to help you get the clearest picture possible of the boxxes that may be holding you back.

Get Out of Your Boxx

The Boxx Of Power And Control

I suspect you all know someone who lives in the Boxx of Power and Control, or maybe you live there yourself. These people attempt to allay their big Boxx of Fear by keeping their thumb on everyone else. Although there may be a variety of issues behind this, the end result is the same. They think they are keeping life safe and secure when, in fact, they frequently cause tremendous turmoil, anger, distrust, and sometimes even hate in those around them.

For example, the boss who just *has* to double check each employee's work because she does not trust their performance, consequently instills in them resentment, fear and a lack of trust in return. While she may think she is keeping everything running smoothly, she is sitting on a powder keg waiting to ignite when they tire of her controlling behaviors. They may quit, or out of spite, intentionally sabotage her at a significant time. All the while, she firmly believes that her Boxx of Power and Control is keeping her safe. However, if she hired competent people and gave them room to work, they would probably be more willing to do a good job because she showed trust in their ability to do so.

Another example of the Boxx of Power and Control backfiring can be seen in relationships. Let's say that your boyfriend is terrified of losing you, thus he attempts to keep you "near and dear to his heart." In other words, he is in the Boxx of Power and Control but his Boxx of Fear of Abandonment is really in charge. He says he loves you more than anything. He worships the ground you walk on. Yet his behavior makes you feel as if he has you on a leash. He wants to know exactly where you are at any given time and who you are with. He feels anxious and lost when you are not with him. He constantly talks about marriage with the unconscious belief that if you are married you won't leave him. He keeps thinking that this behavior will keep him from harm.

So Many Boxxes, So Little Time

Yet, what effect does this behavior have on you? I bet it probably makes you want to run! Look at it this way. If you keep your dog on a leash 24 hours a day, what does he do the second you take him off the leash? More than likely, he runs away! He asserts his freedom. And he becomes increasingly hesitant to return to you if he thinks he must live on that leash every day. However, if you give your dog his freedom each day, care for him lovingly, give him all the things he needs in life, and *show* him your love and affection, I'll bet he will prefer to stay with you rather than be anywhere else. Did you have to assert Power and Control over your dog, or were you better not to? Personally, I'd like knowing that my dog chose to stay with me out of love, not because he was trapped with me!

Some people even have to control the minutia in the lives of those around them. For example, Jim gets incredibly angry if something doesn't go the way he planned. For example, during what should have been a great ski day with his family, he instantly became extremely angry over what should have been nothing. The result – his family spent the rest of the day walking on eggshells around him. Why? Because he got upset when the children changed their minds three times about what time to have lunch! He just couldn't handle the fact that no one respected him as the ultimate control figure of the family, and his feelings were hurt if others' ideas "won out." If he thought he was being safer in his Boxx of Power and Control, he was dead wrong. Inevitably, as these types of behaviors continued, his wife threw in the towel and divorced him. The world he thought he could keep safe through his use of Power and Control rapidly disintegrated before his eyes.

Living in the Boxx of Power and Control is not what it's cracked up to be. It may appear to work for a while, but in the long run it can cause a great deal of pain and trauma for everyone involved.

Get Out of Your Boxx

The Unfulfilled Relationship Boxx

Many people "settle" when they choose a significant other in their life. Or sometimes relationships change, but neither party is willing to recognize that the changes have led to them feeling unfulfilled and empty.

If we remember to take care of ourselves first, and are true to what is important to us, we will never have to find ourselves in this oppressive boxx to begin with. This does *not* mean you are egotistical or conceited. It *does* mean you are true to your beliefs, values, and taking care of your health – emotional as well as physical.

Consider Cindy. She had been dating Rob for nearly two years when she started questioning his motives and behaviors. She told me how she was getting progressively uncomfortable with him and couldn't understand why he had changed. Many of his behaviors had not bothered her at the beginning, when she was falling in love, but she had realized over time that they were not all healthy for her. She had kept wishing and hoping that he would outgrow them as their relationship matured, but she had begun to realize she was only kidding herself. When I asked her why she stayed with him if she wasn't happy, she said, "I've invested all this time in him. I hate to simply walk away now!"

This is the *wrong* reason to stay in any relationship! If you question your feelings about him now, the odds of him changing for the better over the next 10 years are not in your favor. Add to that any major life issues that come along and the situation is likely to explode. If you choose to stay with him because you realize you are at a "bump in the road," and you both agree to work through your issues, then staying makes a great deal of sense. However, don't let yourself get talked into staying in a bad relationship because several years have passed or you see your 25th anniversary looming in the future.

So Many Boxxes, So Little Time

Relationships can make or break our lives. Enjoying people who add joy, trust, caring, love, and any number of other positive emotions to your life is one of our true gifts indeed. There are many special people in the world who can make your life more wonderful. Why would you waste time with those who tear you down, belittle you, abuse you, or otherwise dismiss you as not being valuable?

As a horsewoman, I have ridden a vast number of horses — some wonderful, some a real pain in my butt (literally!) and some who truly wanted to kill me! Then one day I was reading an article in a horse magazine written by an Olympic rider who believed that many of us waste too much time on bad horses. He had watched his Olympic colleague, Denny, spend hour after hour with a rather rogue horse who bucked his brains out each time he tried to ride him. Denny was convinced this horse's *potential* was incredible, but try as he might, he just could not get the horse to work *with* him and not against him. The columnist finally got through to his friend when he said, "Denny, there are millions of horses in the United States alone. Why are you wasting your time on this one?!"

I realize that horses aren't people, *but* if there are other horses out there that are smarter, more understanding, and would be easier to work with, how many wonderful people must be out there as well? How many who would make a perfect match for you and cause less stress in your life? How many who are not trying to buck you off? How many who enjoy working with you and not against you? How many who might make your life absolutely incredible? If you are not with Mr. or Ms. Right, keep your eyes open for them, and don't get stuck in the Victim Boxx with Mr. or Ms. Wrong! *Be true to you first* and recognize that the best partner you have is someone who is true to themselves as well. If you are both taking care of yourselves, you can give your best care to each other as well.

Get Out of Your Boxx

Suicidal Thoughts: The Eternal Boxx

Having been in this terrifying boxx myself, I feel it necessary to address this issue. The Boxx of Suicidal Thoughts is lonely, sad, heavy, empty, ugly, scary, painful, and so much more that I can't even begin to describe. However, I learned two very important lessons being there:

YOU DON'T HAVE TO BE THERE!

"SUICIDE IS A LONG-TERM ANSWER FOR A SHORT-TERM PROBLEM."

I wish I knew where I read that statement, but I don't. Yet, I hope the person who wrote it realizes what a strong impact it had upon me. Let me say it again:

"SUICIDE IS A LONG-TERM ANSWER FOR A SHORT-TERM PROBLEM."

No matter how horrible things may seem, there is always an alternative. For me, it was running away. In fact, one of my boxxes was Claustrophobia. It had always been my Body Armor Boxx that kept me safe whenever I felt trapped. At that moment it sprang into action and told my gut that I had to run away. The space I found gave me time, and distance, and a safe environment to see things more clearly, and with more possibilities. It also helped me see that I *did not* have to live in my Suicidal Thought Boxx anymore.

I am neither a therapist nor an expert concerning suicide. There are many resources available from books, to call-in help lines, to health care providers who can give more psychological information than I. However, from one who has lived in that boxx let me just say this: If you ever find yourself there, you *DO NOT* have to stay in that deep, dark place. Do

So Many Boxxes, So Little Time

ANYTHING you need to get out. Run away. Share your feelings with a friend. Make a call to an anonymous hotline. Just remember, Suicide is the Eternal Boxx from which there is *NO* return. Many people make a suicide attempt in the hopes that someone will hear their cry. They never really mean to go through with it, yet they end up taking their own lives anyway. Remember that there is more than one way to be heard and get help. The world is full of possibilities but you have to get out of your boxxes to find them.

I repeat,

"SUICIDE IS A LONG-TERM ANSWER FOR A SHORT-TERM PROBLEM!"

I cannot stress this enough. I am living proof that there is sunshine after the storm. You just have to keep your eyes open to see the possibilities. But you have to *choose* to take action to get out of this devastating boxx! Believe me – you *CAN DO IT!* I did!

The Boxx Of Depression

Depression has reached epidemic proportions in our society. The money spent on anti-depressants is mind-boggling. What causes all these people to be depressed? You'd have to ask psychological professionals for their insights into that extremely important question.

As I said earlier, I am neither a doctor nor a therapist, so I can't speak to you from those perspectives. However, I can speak to you from my personal experiences. I found that once I got "Out of My Boxx" and started being *true to me* and *taking care of me first,* I no longer fought depression. This may not be the case for you, but what I do suggest is that you consider studying the underlying causes for your depression. Some of the suggestions in Chapter 17 may help you trace the real issues keeping you captive in the Boxx of Depression.

The Boxx Of Health Issues

Health Issue Boxxes include your Current Health, your Past Health, or your Perceived Health. For example, if you are currently fighting cancer it takes over your life. I am not here to say that's right or wrong, just that it does. It is your Current Health. Your Past Health can seem to have a life of its own – even long after the condition is past. I recently met Rebecca who spent 40 minutes explaining how she'd had encephalitis when she was a child. This woman defined her life by her Past Health issues. It gave her a sense of importance at the same time that it kept her stuck as a victim in her boxx. "Perceived Health" issues fall into the category of the hypochondriac.

The important thing to remember about the Boxxes of Health is not to let them *define* you! When you chronically talk about your illness, it *becomes* you. It takes over your life. It limits you. And it may drive those around you *away*, as they grow tired hearing of about it, especially if the issues are Past or Perceived Health stories. In your attempt to gain their attention, you may inadvertently push them away instead. Beware! This boxx can be very deceiving that way!

I am not here to say that you should ignore your health or any issues you are dealing with. Remember your Body Armor — your useful boxx of health care that *is* healthy for you. Be responsible and take care of yourself, but don't let it lock you in such a boxx that you forget to live your life, and you end up trapping others in the boxx with you!

Boxxes Of Pain

Emotional or physical pain can boxx you in so badly that you absolutely cannot function. You may as well be handcuffed, gagged, and blindfolded because severe pain can leave you senseless. This is where "Out of the Boxx" thinking may help you. If traditional remedies do not touch your physical or emotional pain, examine alternative, holistic therapies. Acupressure, acupuncture, hypnosis, massage, herbs, biofeedback, psychic readings, chiropractic adjustment, Reiki, EMDR (Eye Movement Desensitization and Reprocessing), EFT (Emotional Freedom Technique), and a wide variety of other therapies exist throughout this country. As usual, common sense should prevail. If someone suggests you could eliminate chronic headaches by drinking snake venom, I would think twice!

However, what you might not recognize is that many types of pain can be traced to underlying issues that might appear totally unrelated. I will always remember my psychiatric rotation in nursing school. The patient was a 30-year-old woman who had just had a baby and suddenly developed acute asthma. Her friends and family thought she was allergic to the many baby products she was exposed to. However, with diligent psychological support, the origin of the "pain" she was suffering from was uncovered. Surprisingly enough, it had nothing to do with the baby products and everything to do with the baby itself. The underlying cause of her newly acquired asthma was her belief that her husband was angry with her for getting pregnant since they had decided not to have children early in their marriage. When the child was born she believed that her husband was terribly angry and/or disappointed with her, and that he no longer loved her. What she didn't realize was that her husband had changed his view. Somewhere in the process he had decided that being a father wasn't so bad but he hadn't shared his new feelings with her. Once she understood the change in the situation her asthma magically disappeared!

I am not saying that all your pains will suddenly vanish if you find the underlying cause. However, knowing the root

Get Out of Your Boxx

of your deepest issues and doing something about them can unlock some painful emotional issues that may be keeping you locked in your boxx. By finding them and facing them, you may start knocking down the walls of your personal Boxx of Pain.

Boxxes Of Anger, Resentment, And Revenge

"An eye for an eye?" Does it really work that way? Does living in the Boxx of Anger really get you anywhere, or does it limit you in all areas of your life? Remember all these boxxes have their roots in the Boxx of Fear. Ask yourself what you are afraid of and perhaps your anger, resentment, or revenge won't end up taking over your life. The energy you spend being angry could be diverted to something more productive, more satisfying, and lead you toward greater possibilities. Don't let your anger eat you alive or boxx you in. If you do, the person who is leaving you angry holds all the power for as long as you let him.

The Boxx Of Excuses

By living in the Boxx of Excuses you might think you are freeing yourself from taking responsibility but, in fact, you are locking yourself in that boxx and throwing away the key. Hiding behind excuses lets you be a victim and not be the one in charge of your own life. By believing that you come from a family with fat genes you don't have to work to lose weight because it gives you an acceptable excuse. It's just not your fault. By blaming your boss for "making" you have a bad day, you just gave her the power to determine how you feel. Remember – you choose how you respond to any situation. No one can *make* you feel a certain way if you do not choose to do so. When you blame the weather for keeping you from exercising today, you discount your ability to think intelligently and come up with an alternative way to fit your workout in your day.

These are all excuses, and excuses just don't cut it. If you want to live in the Boxx of Excuses that's fine, just don't expect anyone around you to believe you after a while. And don't expect them to sympathize either for they can usually see the truth.

Those who really want something do not *make* excuses, or *take* excuses. They just find a way.

Boxxes And Boxxes And Boxxes

Below is a list of more boxxes you may discover in your investigation. You may think of even more after you study these. Some overlap with others I've already listed, and some may be similar, but they may speak to you differently with these names:

Boxx of Phobias
Boxx of Boredom
Boxx of Habits
Boxx of Impatience
Boxx of The Victim
Boxx of Unhappiness
Boxx of Pessimism
Boxx of Unlucky Me
Boxx of Poor Me
Boxx of Chronic Fatigue
Boxx of Low Expectations
Boxx of The Unloved
Boxx of Dependency
Boxx of Hate
Boxx of Jealousy
Boxx of Misunderstandings
Boxx of Resistance to Change
Boxx of Sloppiness
Boxx of Wishful Thinking
Boxx of Beliefs

Get Out of Your Boxx

Boxx of Sarcasm and Criticism

So many boxxes, so little time...

Remember to determine which boxxes are helping you and which ones limit you, and that *it is your decision to live in them or leave them!*

"Our fears must never hold us back from pursuing our hopes."
John F. Kennedy

Chapter 14
Are You Boxxing With Denial?

Some people hide in the Boxx of Denial. The American Heritage Dictionary defines the word denial as "a refusal to grant the truth of a statement, or an unconscious defense mechanism characterized by refusal to acknowledge painful realities, thoughts, or feelings."

I think living in this boxx is one of the saddest conditions of all. It's certainly one of the most difficult boxxes to climb out of. Denying that we have anything to work on causes us to miss out on so much and limits the wonderful possibilities that might come our way, were we open enough to see them. Day after day. Year after year. Sameness upon sameness. Think of it like this — if you stayed in the second grade and all your friends kept moving up each year, wouldn't your growth be stunted? Wouldn't you miss out on a lot of possibilities that life offers? By burying your head in the sand and denying that you have anything to improve upon, you lose sight of everything from the simple pleasure of spending more time with your loved ones, to missing out on a big promotion. How so?

Well, what if you are denying that you live in the Workaholic Boxx? Year after year you spend 60 hours a week at the office, convinced that you're "really not working that much." What if one day you realize that your children are grown and on their way to college and you don't even know what their favorite activity is? Or what if they don't want to spend any time with you because you've locked yourself away from them for so long that they don't know who you are either? How many of their events did you miss because you were working? I'll bet your kids could tell you the exact number.

What if the Weighty Boxx limits your physical abilities and you cannot apply for the job you really want because there are physical performance expectations that you cannot meet?

What if you are the hotel cleaning lady and you lose your job because by living in the Perfect Boxx, you can't do an efficient job of cleaning?

If you find yourself in any of these situations, it could be because you have been living in the Boxx of Denial – denying you have anything to work on. Remember, seeing our own reflection in the mirror is sometimes not easy or pleasant. But it may be crucial if you are going to get the things you want from life.

If you want to change behaviors that do not serve you well, you must first identify the boxxes you live in by studying yourself in detail to determine which behaviors are productive and which are not. Even minor issues can play a huge role in your life, as well as the lives of those around you. Hitting that snooze button several times each morning might not bother you, but it might drive your spouse crazy. Instead of hiding your head in the pillow to avoid it, try recognizing that your overworked alarm clock is throwing you a major red flag that something isn't working quite right in your life! Are you getting the message?

On the other hand, there are some people who are always seeking to make themselves better. They regularly attend motivational or self-improvement seminars, take classes on a variety of subjects, read the latest best-seller about some new idea that everyone is talking about. These people have made a conscious decision to grow and learn and change with the ever-changing world. They continuously study their boxxes and issues, with the intention of always striving to be better. You probably know someone like this. They have energy, enthusiasm, rarely get upset, and always seem to get the "lucky breaks." Yet, luck rarely has anything to do with it. They just choose to discover who they are and then make the changes they want. Are you one of these visionaries, or are you stuck in the Boxx of Denial?

Laura

In my travels I've met a lot of people who were Boxxing with Denial. One woman I know, I'll call her Laura, describes herself as a "functioning alcoholic." I guess by that she means that she drinks too much but makes it to work every day. She believes her drinking is "not that bad," and doesn't adversely affect her life in any way. She finds comfort in alcohol – perhaps to cope with any number of boxxes she lives with. Since liquor is generally socially acceptable, she doesn't see it as an addiction in the way that she views marijuana or other illegal substances. And so she drinks – a lot.

What she doesn't see is how it affects so many aspects of her life – her career, her relationships with others, and her health. Her friends at work smell the alcohol on her breath every morning. Sometimes they cover for her, as she gulps coffee to wake up and shake off the hangover. One day they may finally decide they have covered for her long enough, and she will have to suffer the consequences. She rationalizes that since she works in an office, it's not like she is making life and death decisions. Yet, what happens when she's behind the wheel of a car? How many highway deaths occur each year when the Lauras of the world get behind the wheel, believing that they are "functioning alcoholics"?

In her relationships, her friends are always on edge. They never know what to expect when they get together. Is she already drunk, or will it be a good evening at the beginning, fading throughout the night? They may spend much less time with her than they might if she were sober. They are extremely familiar with her changes in behavior as the alcohol takes effect. She gets loud, is uninhibited to the point of calling people names, or shuts down, giving them the "silent treatment," acting hurt if no one pays her enough attention. Being inside the effects of alcohol, she can't see the mirror reflecting the uncomfortable faces around her. Over time, as her friends slowly back away and find new friends, she may be left wondering how she got there. Her friends, of course, might have spent a great deal of time attempting to approach her with their concerns about her drinking. But her Boxx of Denial has her trapped in a place she is not anxious to leave, and she brushes them off, explaining how she's "just fine, thank you very much!"

Of course, her health will take a significant toll in the long run. There is no doubt what effect alcohol has on the body. Unfortunately, unlike a sudden heart attack, which might prove a wake-up call to its recipient, the long slow destruction of a liver never seems to capture the same urgency and need for change. And so Laura will keep on drinking for years, oblivious to the Boxx of Denial where she is held prisoner by her own choice.

Chris

Another captive of this boxx is Chris. She is a professional businesswoman in her early 40s. I suspect she was probably a cheerleader in high school, as she has one of those extremely outgoing, bubbly personalities. She's got beautiful blue eyes and a wonderful smile, but behind that animated mask she lives in some pretty tight boxxes. She is probably 75 pounds overweight, drinks heavily, and talks incessantly about the "hundreds" of boyfriends she's had. (Although she never mentions one meaningful relationship.) She also loves to brag about the money she makes and her "Lexus" lifestyle, since she has a high-powered job with a big company. She thoroughly enjoys gossiping about everybody and telling incredible stories about her wild adventures at every party, every weekend. Yet, she goes home to an empty house and unfulfilled love and proclaims, "There's nothing wrong with me!"

What do these women have in common? They are in denial about their real issues. Perhaps loneliness, depression, a sense of dissatisfaction with their life choices, or poor self-esteem. It's hard to know precisely, yet their behaviors reflect more than what they recognize. Those of us on the outside can see how desperately they are struggling with issues of some sort that are neither productive nor satisfying and may, in fact, be destructive.

I still struggle with my own boxxes. I have not yet escaped from all of them completely, but I have started to recognize them and do something about them. I still battle small boxxes of Claustrophobia, Fear of Failure, and especially Impatience. I don't mind that my Claustrophobic Boxx still keeps me from scuba diving in caves, which is an adventure I can choose to live without! However, if I'm not careful it can also let me fall into my self-protective mode in my relationships with others. Holding myself hostage in that boxx does nothing to evolve and improve those situations. There are times I have to consciously realize that I'm about to run away when things get too confining, and I need to turn myself around immediately before I miss out on opportunities for growth and other wonderful things.

When I began to date again after my divorce, I found it very easy to pull back and slam doors on men I thought were interested in "trapping" me with their expectations of what a girlfriend should be. If they didn't treat me exactly the way I envisioned, I shut the door on them out of fear – fear of being trapped in a confining relationship in which I felt I had no control. I believed that it was safer for me to simply close the door than to take a risk and give the relationship some time to evolve and allow discovery of what each person truly brought to the table. In my willingness to run for cover at the first sign of entrapment, I nearly missed some great possibilities that came my way. Over time, by taking baby-step risks, I gradually came out of my self-limiting Claustrophobic Boxx and experimented with new behaviors that led me to a different path. With each new, small success, I gained sufficient ground and trust that not everyone wanted to lock me into a given role and that, in fact, a good relationship was achievable.

The biggest boxx I lived in for so many years was the Unfulfilled, Empty Boxx. At the time I lived in this confusing place, I was living in my own Boxx of Denial. On the outside I thought I seemed pretty "together," at least that's what my friends always told me. I functioned. I got up every day. I took care of my family. I rode and competed in horse shows. I wore a pretty good mask. I fooled everybody — or at least I thought I did. In truth, that boxx left its mark on so many aspects of my life. It left me with symptoms of depression, chronic fatigue, back pain, and headaches. I needed 10 to 12 hours of sleep each day, and still felt drained. Getting out of bed in the morning was a chore. I even questioned my value in life.

How did I climb out of this very painful and confining boxx? I finally realized I needed to make some serious changes in my life. First, I left an unfulfilling relationship. That alone, allowed me to start being true to my inner desires. My sabbatical in Mexico gave me time and space to think more clearly. Over time, I began to realize that the two things I had been most passionate about for years were writing and helping people. From there, it was a matter of choosing the path that felt right for me. I journaled my heart out in Mexico, letting thoughts and feelings pour out in a way I had never experienced before. This certainly was the spark for my new career in writing columns and books. I began to remember how passionate I was about public speaking and started exploring avenues where I could use that God-given talent in a way that

Are You Boxxing With Denial?

would provide me excitement and satisfaction. Thus, Out of the Boxx, Inc. was born. If I hadn't quit denying that I was tragically locked in my boxxes, I would have never taken that leap of faith and jumped out of my boxxes with both feet – despite my fears. By facing my boxxes head-on, I was able to see their effects on me and could start tearing them down, piece by piece, to reveal so many unknown possibilities that changed my life.

Examine your life. What do you really see? Is the Boxx of Denial limiting your potential or your possibilities? You don't have to take a sabbatical, but you can make other changes in your life. Remember, *you have the power* to make changes, but first you must recognize your boxxes before you can change them! So get out your sledge hammer and start tearing them down right now, before you change your mind!

"Successful people are always looking for opportunities to help others. Unsuccessful people are always asking "What's in it for me?"

Brian Tracey – motivational speaker.

Get Out of Your Boxx

Part Three
Trapped By Someone Else's Boxx

Sometimes we get caught up in boxxes that aren't even our own. They really belong to someone else but they seem like ours, and we embrace them as if they belong to us. It can be just as hard, or even harder, to break out of these boxxes as those we truly own, but it can be done. However, discovering that your issues belong to someone else may actually make it easier to understand your feelings and behaviors, and can lead you to take steps to free yourself from the weight of pressure and stress that is not yours to begin with. You may just feel like you have been set free from indentured servitude when you are finished!

"Freedom's just another word for nothin' left to lose."

Janice Joplin

Chapter 15
The Expectations Of Others

In the small town I grew up in, one of the phrases I learned early on was, "What will the neighbors say?" When everyone knows everyone in a small, conservative, mid-western town, the neighbors' opinions somehow seemed to carry more weight than my own. Views on such things as how much makeup someone wore, how short their skirts were, or who they were dating always seemed to be up for public debate. At least that's what it felt like as a kid. Although I live outside of Denver now, and the small-town atmosphere is no longer an issue, I've found that I still have a lot of friends who make their life choices based upon the Expectations of Others or, more specifically, what someone else would say or think. And for the longest time, I did too.

I still fell victim to the Boxx of the Expectation of Others about the time I decided to run away from home and go to Mexico. When I made arrangements to leave my house, my horses, and my dog with various friends during my adventure I never dreamed I would have so many people give me their "two cents worth" about my plans, nor how much pressure I felt from their comments. One friend said, "I don't know how you can leave your daughter like that." At that time, my daughter was living in the dormitory at college and was quite busy with her new life, her boyfriend, and her classes. She certainly wasn't spending her time with me. Had she gone out of state to school, as many children do, she wouldn't have had me nearby to begin with.

Another person questioned, "Why can't you wait a while? I don't understand why you have to go now." Since one of the things I was trying to avoid was the gloom and cold of winter, it seemed to make much more sense to leave in January rather than in April. Why should I wait? Wait for what? In truth, what they were really hoping was that I would just change my mind and be "my old self" again.

My very part-time job at the time was teaching horseback riding lessons at a local barn. I was especially surprised when my boss, one of the few people who seemed to actually understand how depressed and desperate I was, remarked, "How can you leave the students like this? They depend upon you!" Since there were other instructors who could take over my students, and since winter is the slow season in the riding business, I wasn't sure why she wanted me to feel guilty about my decision. I also knew that if any of those students decided to switch barns and take lessons with another instructor, they certainly wouldn't have felt too guilty leaving me! Everyone has to live their life the way they see fit and those types of choices are made every day. My students were my clients, not my offspring.

Even more interesting was the reception I received from some people after my return home from my six months away. I emailed a group of social friends to tell them I was home and was shocked when almost no one responded. I couldn't understand what had happened.

At last, a friend of mine said something that made sense. She told me I had changed, and my friends didn't know what to do with me. I no longer fit into the nice, neat boxxes they expected me to. I broke the rules and left my confining boxxes that had held me captive, and had gone to live in Paradise. It was as if some of them felt justified punishing me for my behavior. Since they were still in their ruts, they expected I should be too. Perhaps the Boxxes of Jealousy or Resentment

The Expectations of Others

were locking some in their ruts. Or maybe it was just that since I had moved out of their lives, they had found other people to replace me. That part I understood completely, but I didn't understand the silent treatment.

It was then I began to understand more clearly the issues that go along with the Expectations of Others Boxx. At first I had feelings of guilt, shame, doubt, rejection, and confusion. Some of these same people no longer seemed interested in being my friends, and I was hurt. Yet, after a while I began to realize that, in part, it was the changes in me that left others confused. They wanted me to be the "same old, same old person" and I wasn't. The wonderful, unanticipated result was that as some of these people seemed to move out of my life, others took their place. New people who related better to the "new" me suddenly seemed to appear. I discovered people who were more open-minded to the things I was doing with my life, who were interested in the idea of living "Out of the Boxx." In fact, some were already living their lives that way. Their energy and self-direction meshed with my own and together we imagined even greater ideas and possibilities in our incredible life journeys. We made each other better.

Does the Expectations of Others Boxx hold you captive? Perhaps you are still hearing your mother's voice when you get dressed in the morning, "You should never wear anything with horizontal stripes. It makes you look fat." Or maybe your colleague's voice rings in your ears every time you start your taxes, "You don't have a lick of sense when it comes to numbers."

Or how about when you decide to spend your money on a new car? You've worked your heart out for this purchase and planned your money carefully. You have your mind set on a black sedan and have had it clearly pictured in your dreams for months. Finally, the day you decide to order it, your spouse says, "Gee, doesn't black fade awfully fast in the sun? Maybe you should pick silver instead." Who do you listen to?

Get Out of Your Boxx

Your own voice, or that off-hand comment made by someone else? Do you get sucked into someone else's Boxx of Conservatism? Let's say you take the safe route and buy the silver one. How will you feel about it for years to come? Will you thank your spouse for his or her wisdom, or will you kick yourself every time you look at that car and wish you had gotten black? If you went with silver and are not happy with your decision, you may have gotten boxxed in by the Expectations of Others.

How many of us make some or many of our life decisions based upon what other people think? Probably more than we realize.

I remember deciding to write a children's book several years ago. The day I made that decision I couldn't wait to tell my husband. We had gone out to lunch and he had been telling me about a big project going on at his office while we were reading our menus. When there was an appropriate break in the conversation, I made my announcement. I was going to write a book! I held my breath, waiting for his reply, and when none came, I hesitatingly asked if he had heard me. He nodded, still reading his menu, and said, "Yes, I heard you. I'll just believe it when I see it."

Those few words held a power over me which has been hard to shake off to this day. As it turned out, I put hours into that book and the 120 pages I completed years ago still sit on my bookshelf. I know exactly what needs to go in to the last three chapters to finish it, but my interest got pulled in other directions. On one hand, it doesn't bother me because I know when I decide to finish it, the job won't be complicated. On the other hand, something still holds me back from finishing that book. Was it his comment, "I'll believe it when I see it?." Did I allow him to predict my demise before I started? Am I still living my life based upon his expectations of me and am I living in his Boxx of Pessimism?

The Expectations of Others

Perhaps part of my mission in writing "Get Out of Your Boxx…" is to free myself from *his* boxx once and for all. I did almost let myself get momentarily sidetracked by another friend and her expectations at one point. I had sent her several chapters of this book to review as I was writing it, and told her that I was determined to complete the first draft the following week, to which she said, "Well, I've heard that before." For a moment I could feel her expectations beginning to seep over me like a heavy fog, but I caught myself in time to remember that it was not her life, or her book, or her mission. It was mine. She didn't walk in my shoes – only I did. Whether I finished the book or not was *my* decision.

One day I had another epiphany. A small one at best, but a light bulb went on in my head and I stopped to ask myself a question. If I were to fall into a coma that left me unconscious for six months, how many people in my world would drop everything to be with me? Who would visit me daily? Who would watch over me throughout my ordeal? Certainly my mother, daughter, and sister. Beyond that, others would stop by occasionally, but probably no one else would dedicate their lives to caring for me unconditionally. With this information, I began to look at people differently. Why would I worry about what the "neighbors" think if they are not significant players in my life to begin with? Since they wouldn't be part of my inner crowd of support people, why should their opinion matter regarding my life decisions? Unless I am affecting their lives in some way, or breaking a law, their opinion should certainly carry less weight than my own. It was a very liberating moment indeed.

Even when it comes to those in my inner circle, they still cannot live my life for me. They cannot feel my feelings, know my innermost thoughts, or walk in my shoes. As long as I am honest and true to them, love them unconditionally, give myself fully to the relationship, and know and respect their feelings, I am not obligated to live in their Boxxes of Expectations of *me*. For example, if I grew up in a family where everyone became doctors, but I wanted to be a writer, should I become a doctor just because that was the expectation of those around me? Does it make more sense for me to make everyone around me happy and not be true to myself? In the long run would I resent them for "making" me become a doctor and cheating me out of my own dreams? This is where the Expectations of Others can get confusing and oppressive, and send your life spiraling in directions you may not want to go.

Another realization came to me as a result of my earlier belief that the Expectations of Others should carry an enormous amount of weight and power. I had volunteered for years with my daughter's equestrian organization, had been the leader of the club (which encompassed thousands of hours of phone calls, mailings, meetings, organization, etc.), gave free lessons to many of the kids in my back yard, allowed them to borrow my equipment, and even let them use my horses on occasion. I guess I wanted them to like me and, as a result, believed that these behaviors won me "places of honor" in their minds. If anyone ever needed a favor, they only needed to ask me.

However, when I decided to turn professional, and began teaching riding lessons at a local barn where I was paid for my services, things suddenly changed. The club, now under new leadership, was no longer interested in my services. They searched for someone new to hire as one of their paid instructors. Needless to say, my ego was shattered. By giving of myself for years, I had believed I had won their admiration and respect. And yet, what I learned was that their expectations were completely wrapped up in my services being "free." For the longest time I was crushed. I felt angry, hurt, sad, disappointed, useless, devalued, and any other negative adjective that might jump into my brain. What was worse was that it all took place at the same time the other overwhelming issues were going on in my life. My beliefs of being valuable to oth-

The Expectations of Others

ers became totally scrambled with my belief of being valuable to myself. The end result was that I couldn't find my value anywhere.

What did this lesson teach me? That it is extremely easy to get sucked up into the Boxxes of Others' Expectations and it becomes vital to recognize which boxxes are mine and which belong to someone else. Had I been able to realize that I had given of myself for the wrong reasons to begin with — seeking my own validation through the praise of others — I would have been better able to predict the response I received. Or at least I would not have been so surprised by it.

Having come to understand that "what the neighbors say" need not have power and control over my life, has helped me to see what is important to me — to my health, my relationships, and my career. Being *true to me first*, and *taking care of me first*, are both my responsibilities and my freedoms. I have realized that I can still care for and love the others in my life in a way that does not boxx me into the wrong boxxes based upon *their* expectations. Understanding this now has helped me to become a stronger person — healthier, happier, and better able to handle whatever life events come along. At the same time, it is important for me to remember it is not my place to put *my* expectations upon others in my life, which may be an even more difficult task at times!

Ask yourself, why does it matter what others think of your behaviors or beliefs? You are the only one whose opinion should really matter. Are you taking care and being true to yourself first? Or are you walled up in the Boxx of the Expectations of Others?

It is important, however, that you still need to be responsible and accountable. For me to escape to Mexico at a time when I had no one else to care for was a safe and organized decision. If you believe you need *only* listen to your inner voice and run away from home, leaving your spouse with a new baby and a mortgage he can't pay for on his own, then

Get Out of Your Boxx

that is *not* responsible behavior. In this case, what your spouse thinks definitely has impact upon your decision! However, by thinking "Outside the Boxx" you might be able to come up with some alternatives to caring for yourself and being true to what you are passionate about without actually running away from home! However, if as a family you decide to move to a small town in Wyoming to raise your kids but your neighbors think you're crazy, who cares what your neighbors think?! Tell them it's your life and to get over it!

If you think you are still getting boxxed in by the Expectations of Others, ask yourself the following questions, remembering they are only a starting place. You can develop others that may let you see yourself more clearly:

- ❑ Do you wonder what others think and say about your weight or your looks?
- ❑ Do you worry what your parents or siblings think about your behaviors or choices?
- ❑ Do you worry that people won't like you if you don't do something their way?
- ❑ Do you keep your opinions to yourself for fear others won't agree with you, or may criticize you for your views?
- ❑ Do you dress to please others in your life, yet you are uncomfortable in those clothes?
- ❑ Do you always rely on someone else to tell you how to think, feel, or believe about an issue?
- ❑ Do you have a superficial relationship with someone because you are afraid to tell them the truth about something they do that bothers you?
- ❑ Do you dislike certain people but keep them in your social circle because you feel obligated to do so?
- ❑ Are you afraid to stand up to someone because you fear they might reject you or dislike you?
- ❑ Are you fulfilling someone else's desires and not

The Expectations of Others

- Are you who you truly want to be, or are you living your life the way those around you "expect" you to live?
- Do you readily believe the opinions of your spouse, parents, friends, colleagues, or supervisors when they say you are a bad parent, friend, employee, or spouse?
- Do you spend all your extra money on your kids and rarely on yourself because parents are always supposed to come last?
- Do you fall prey to the social expectation that a "good mother" stays home with her growing children rather than work outside the home?
- Do you believe that in a strong relationship neither partner should ever need time alone? That if you really love each other you should spend all of your time together?
- Do you think others are smarter or better than you?
- Do you believe men are smarter than women or vice versa?

Remember, studying yourself in detail can be difficult. There is a fine line between being selfish and *taking care of* yourself.

When I began to develop my Out of the Boxx company and decided I wanted to teach seminars to help others think "Outside the Boxx," an acquaintance challenged me saying, "What credentials do you have that entitle you to teach such a course? Who's going to want to listen to you anyway?" At the time she made the remark, I had two choices. Either I could let myself believe her criticism and question my value, which could have caused me to abort my plans altogether, or I could recognize that what she thought didn't make a difference to me. I chose the second. While I did stop to evaluate the accuracy of her message, I realized that even though I didn't have a doctorate in psychology, nor was I educated as a life coach, perhaps the things I bring to the table were different than the typical therapist or coach and valuable in other ways. There are thousands of people with professional training who offer standard classes and support to their clients. What I felt I offered was a view from another perspective. Of course, the fact that I had a master's degree in nursing didn't hurt, but more importantly, I had lived through some of the worst depths and greatest highs possible in life. I had survived abuse, an unsatisfying marriage, a turbulent divorce, raising a child to adulthood, a close brush with suicide, running away from home as an adult (which had proven to be the best thing I ever did for myself), changing careers several times, and now I was enmeshed in my philosophy of living my life "Out of the Boxx."

What were my credentials? Well, perhaps by surviving many life challenges that any therapist or coach might have learned about through educational and theoretical means, I could give my clients a different perspective on their issues. Maybe people would want to listen to me since they knew I understood their pain first-hand. Perhaps my message would touch the lives of some who had never found their direction in the usual places. After all, how many therapists or coaches do you know who actually ran away from home as an adult, and not only lived to tell about it, but who changed their life completely afterwards? While I believe wholeheartedly in professionals to help people in a variety of ways, (one certainly helped me profoundly,) I also believe in looking "Outside the Boxx" for other supportive avenues as well. Being able to relate to someone who has experienced similar circumstances is a way to form a bond unlike many others.

I could have listened to "what the neighbors think" in my colleague's statement. However, I listened to me instead. Had I fallen into the Boxx of the Expectation of Others, I

The Expectations of Others

would be in a completely different place now. I know I wouldn't be as passionate about life as I am. I wouldn't be as excited about what each new day might bring. And I'm convinced I wouldn't be as happy. I certainly wouldn't have written this book!

The other thing I have chosen to do is to eliminate as many negative people from my life as possible. Their negativism never brings anyone around them "up" but most definitely brings *everyone* down. When you surround yourself with cheerleaders, you are more motivated to win. Why do you think cheerleaders have been a cornerstone of organized sports for so long?

So find yourself some cheerleaders, clear out the negative influences in your life, and quit worrying about "what the neighbors say." Keep in mind that we all tend to live in enough of our own boxxes to begin with; it doesn't help to take on anyone else's! So why not give them back to whomever they belong to?

"Reputation is what you are perceived to be. Character is what you are."

John Wooden

Chapter 16
Narcissism — Boxxed In By The "Master Of The Universe"

Do you know someone who is in a relationship where he or she feels totally unequal to their partner? Where one person feels so much less important than the other? Where one continually tries to make the other happy, but no matter what they do it is never good enough or perfect enough? Does one person always feel like a failure in the relationship and blame themselves for things going badly? Well, there's a good chance he or she is involved with a narcissist.

The term "narcissism" comes from the mythological story of a Greek youth named Narcissus who rejected the romantic advances of a nymph named Echo. As punishment for his behavior he was cursed to fall in love with his own reflection in a pool of water. He was so infatuated with his image that he was unable to leave it, and eventually died on the spot, where he was mystically transformed into the flower still bearing his name today.

Most narcissists (75 percent) are men. Adolph Hitler comes to mind as perhaps the best known and most extreme narcissist. Certainly, most are not as lethal or as famous. However, there are many other small-scale narcissists in our society who inflict their own level of damage upon those they live with, trapping their victims in boxxes of guilt, fear, shame, and self-doubt, to name but a few.

The most commonly recognizable examples of narcissists are abusive husbands. Whether physically, sexually, or emotionally abusive, they are the ones we see on television and in movies wrecking havoc upon those around them. *Sleeping With The Enemy* and *Enough* are both movies portraying husbands with deep seated narcissistic behaviors. Both husbands exhibited absolute power and control over every aspect of their wives' lives while inflicting abuse as "punishment" for perceived poor performance of any kind. This type of relationship is dangerous, and professional help should be sought at the earliest possible sign. Abuse, whether physical, sexual or emotional, is not acceptable in any relationship! Remember, taking care of *you* first is crucial, especially in these situations, and even more so when children are involved. Do *not* feel responsible for the abuse you receive. It is the abuser's boxx, not yours.

Equally destructive, but with a different approach, are the many narcissists who live quietly in all areas of society. I'll call them "stealth narcissists." Some are highly respectable members of our communities, often appearing to be wonderful people. They are executives of big companies, media personalities, or successful business people. On the outside they may wear a mask of sincerity, kindness, friendliness, and of being a genuinely nice person. They may belong to civic organizations and donate hours of volunteer time to help others. Their public demeanor demonstrates extreme competence, compassion, understanding, and/or a great sense of humor. They may give their time and resources in a manner that seems completely humanitarian. Yet beneath this veneer lies a personality that can inflict extreme damage upon others.

Although they may appear extremely self-confident and sometimes egotistical, in fact, just the opposite is true. Their inner self is full of fear and self-loathing, believed to have begun in childhood when certain needs of love and compassion were not provided. They do not love themselves, nor do they know how to love anyone else. Yet, by wearing the mask of

"Master of the Universe" they believe they excel at whatever they attempt. From there they begin to believe they are God-like and others are only here to meet their needs. This façade allows them to be on the offensive rather than the defensive.

They love to be admired and adored by others and will find a way to meet that need at all costs – even if they have to play a role they might disdain in order to achieve it. They fall into two categories: 1) Somatic — depicted by physical prowess or accomplishment such as body building, sexual claims, or pure physical attractiveness, or 2) Cerebral — demonstrated by their intellectual brilliance. No matter which type, when their needs are not met to the degree they deem appropriate, they feel justified in punishing those who are responsible.

Unfortunately, the reality is that no one can *ever* make them happy as they are not happy with themselves to begin with. Anyone attempting to make these people happy is on an endless mission that will always fail. This vicious cycle is self-perpetuating. The more the "victim" tries to please the narcissist and fails, the stronger become the feelings of low self-esteem in the victim. She then believes she is to blame for the problems and that the narcissist has every right to be disappointed or angry with her performance. The end result is that the victim is held captive in one of many boxxes not truly belonging to her, wondering how she got there. As her self-esteem continues to be eroded, she develops a stronger belief that her narcissistic partner is right and that she is incapable of living without his direction and supreme intellect. He is indeed the "Master of her Universe." How could she possibly function without him?

This type of victim is portrayed by Allison Janney in the movie *American Beauty*. Janney's character is the wife of the narcissistic, military man. As a result of years of living with her domineering husband, she has the "deer in the headlights" look throughout the movie. Looking into her eyes one gets the feeling that no one is home. She has been berated for so long that she no longer fights her situation, believing that she is as unimportant as the furniture. This dangerous boxx is the unwitting result of the quiet or "stealth narcissist" – one who may look very much like Mr. Right to the outside world but who can prove to be very much Mr. Wrong for his partner.

Of course, some narcissists are women. Years ago in Colorado a high ranking military officer attempted to kill his wife when she was in the hospital by injecting a toxic substance into her intravenous line. Caught in the act, the military wasted no time in court-martialing him for "conduct unbecoming an officer." The stranger part of the story, however, was that the man claimed his wife had abused him for years, and his defense was that he had finally "snapped" under the pressure.

A woman I know named Jackie runs her household with an iron fist. Her husband and children are terrified of her and she wears no mask to hide her true self – she is the Almighty in her house and what she says is Gospel. While she believes she is respected and loved by her family members, she is feared and loathed instead. Her children count the days until they are old enough to escape her domination. Her husband, however, has become a puppet, jumping and asking "how high" whenever she barks. This is *not* a healthy boxx, and those who continue to live in it develop lifelong scars to show as a result. They may become sarcastic, negative, abusive, withdrawn, frightened, shy, or rebellious. They may even build a similarly narcissistic environment for their own children, thus perpetuating the cycle.

I met three women last year who helped me realize just how powerful the "stealth narcissist" can be in a person's life, and just how detrimental. These are their stories.

Irene

Irene was a 40-year-old black woman who was vice president of a bank in a big city. She successfully managed 65

Get Out of Your Boxx

people and millions of dollars, was the president of several professional organizations, was a pillar of the community, and was respected by many. In her career, she was extremely successful, having worked her way up the ranks one step at a time. She went to work excited to see what she could accomplish each day. Yet, there was another side to Irene's life. What she told me next made me sad, as I could see the pain and confusion in her face as she told the personal side of her story.

She had been married for 20 years to a successful businessman who owned several shops throughout the community. They had two great teenage boys and the family had a substantial income. Yet, despite all these seemingly wonderful things, Irene was miserable. She told me the minute she walked into her own house at the end of the day she felt two inches tall. Her husband, a classic narcissist, reminded her on a regular basis just how incompetent she was. She didn't cook right. Didn't keep the house clean enough. Certainly didn't make love adequately or often enough. No matter what she did, it was never enough. She described one particular day when she was about to take the boys to soccer practice. At the last moment, she had to return unexpectedly to retrieve something from the bedroom she shared with her husband. There she found him vacuuming the tops of the curtains, furious with her that she had enough time to take the boys to soccer but not to vacuum the tops of the curtains! Although he was never physically or verbally abusive, his constant criticism and controlling behaviors kept her locked in boxxes of self-doubt, fear, shame, sadness, depression, anger, resentment and emptiness. Despite all her great career accomplishments, nothing she did mattered in her husband's eyes. He considered her no better than a servant, and a useless one at that, when she didn't meet all his needs instantly and to his liking.

As she told me this story, tears streamed down her face in total confusion and despair. How could she be so successful in her career while at the same time be such a "failure" as a person? What she didn't understand was no matter what she did, she would never be able to please her husband because deep inside of him he was unable to find satisfaction with himself to begin with. The result, her Mr. Right was tearing her apart in her efforts to win his approval, and was a definite Mr. Wrong for her long-term, emotional health.

Julia

I met Julia when she and her boyfriend Fred were on vacation in Cozumel. They were both in their late 30s and had lived together for several years. Fred hoped that Julia would marry him. She was a very short woman and he, an extremely tall man. Their dramatic difference in size was just as symbolic as their inequality in the relationship. While on vacation, they decided to take the Introduction to Scuba Diving class offered by the hotel's dive shop. I was free that afternoon and decided to join them on their dive and I arrived on the scene as their lesson in the pool was coming to a close. There were four couples in the pool with two dive instructors, and they were all practicing their underwater skills, getting comfortable with the equipment.

Suddenly, Julia and Fred surfaced while the others continued practicing. Julia was sputtering and panicking as she realized she was not the least bit comfortable with the situation. She pulled off her mask and began to babble to Fred about how she felt panicked, that she just "couldn't do it." As she sobbed, her words began to suggest more than simple fear of diving. She gripped Fred's arm pathetically, begging him to continue the dive without her as she "knew he would enjoy it." But the last thing she begged was, "Please, Fred, *please* don't be mad at me."

The look of sheer disgust on his face told me that what she had feared the most — his disappointment with her — had already occurred. I saw her shrink emotionally before my eyes. Had she been in a relationship of unconditional love — a relationship where caring, compassion, empathy and understanding were regularly practiced and demonstrated, this woman would never have had to "fear" her partner's reaction. Yet, why didn't she get compassion and understanding from him? Why didn't he support her in her decision not to go ahead with the dive? My guess is that his narcissistic tendencies had already taught her that it was *her* responsibility to meet his expectations and his needs, and when she didn't meet the mark, it was *her* fault.

When she saw me on the side of the pool she came up to me and started apologizing for her "incompetence" all over again. Recognizing her situation, I immediately reassured her that diving isn't a sport for everyone and that it was perfectly OK for her to back out of something she was uncomfortable with, especially since she was uncomfortable in only three feet of water. I knew that 40 feet was not going to be better! She hesitatingly questioned, "Well, do you think it's OK if I come back and try it again tomorrow?"

I reassured her and told her that if she felt a continued interest she could surely try again the next day. However, I suggested that she not bring her boyfriend. She had been unable to see the pressure he had put upon her to "perform." I hoped that without him she could relax enough to learn the scuba skills calmly without his condescending attitude. She would be one-on-one with an instructor who had frequently helped people with similar fears. The end result was that she did come back for another lesson – without the critical boyfriend – and she mastered the skills, allowing them to dive together later in the day. The Boxx of Fear holding Julia captive was due to Fred's controlling, narcissistic behavior, stripping her of her ability to determine her own capabilities in the situation. Yet she did not readily recognize how his Boxx of Narcissism was not her own.

Is this Mr. Right or Mr. Wrong? It becomes clear that physical or sexual abuse need not play a role in every harmful relationship, but the emotional abuse one carries from situations like this leaves their scars, nonetheless.

Bobbie

The last woman I met was a critical care nurse from Texas. She and her son were vacationing in Cozumel over the holidays and when I asked her if her husband had stayed at the hotel instead of going on the day tour she and her son had taken, she told me he never vacationed with them. He couldn't be bothered to go places with them or do things they liked to do. He just lived in front of his computer all day, ruling his domain as he deemed fit.

Then she shared with me that she was waiting, just biding her time for one more year until her son graduated from high school, at which point she was planning to leave her husband. As she told me about some of his behaviors, I could understand why. He insisted the house be spotless and nothing be out of place. She told me about one particular incident where she was preparing an educational demonstration for the new nurses who had just started their careers in the Intensive Care Unit where she was the educator. The day before her presentation she was at home practicing her speech and had laid out all the items she would need to teach the class on her kitchen counter, including syringes, tape, and other nursing equipment. In the middle of her rehearsal, she stopped for a short bathroom break. To her surprise when she returned, all of her items had disappeared! She discovered that her husband had wandered into the kitchen, and upon finding the display of "disallowed" items on "his" counter, had promptly thrown them all in the trash!

Although we were interrupted and I didn't hear the rest of the story, the one thing this woman demonstrated throughout was defiance. She was strong within herself and had already begun to make her plans for the future. How she maintained her confidence and drive was unclear to me, but she had decided not to let herself get walled up in the Boxx of Narcissism. She was gathering her ammunition to be ready when the time was right.

Did all these women recognize Mr. Wrong from the beginning? Of course not. One amazing characteristic of a narcissist is that he knows how to play the role of the charming, caring, kind, compassionate partner during the courting phase of any relationship. They are the "great pretenders" or chameleons while they search for a mate. Since they can oftentimes go unrecognized by professional therapists, the general public can easily be fooled as well. Thus begins the road down the path of narcissism. Once caught up in the web of confusion, the victim doesn't even know what hit her and more problematically, doesn't know how to get out.

The following is a list of behaviors frequently found in narcissists. These may help you to see more clearly if you are living in your own boxxes or those perpetuated by a narcissist in your life.

- ❏ Extreme infatuation with oneself
- ❏ Constant need for admiration or approval
- ❏ Exaggerates personal achievements while minimizing those of others
- ❏ Convinced that he or she is unique
- ❏ Feels entitled to special treatment and that rules frequently don't apply to them
- ❏ Demands compliance with his or her expectations
- ❏ Is unable to show empathy or compassion
- ❏ Does not seem to feel real happiness or positive emotions
- ❏ Criticizes others often
- ❏ Assumes himself to be more knowledgeable than those around him
- ❏ Rages with anger or inflicts the "silent treatment" when upset

Narcissism: Boxxed In By The "Master Of The Universe"

- ❑ Denies he has issues to work on – sees himself as nearly perfect
- ❑ Likes to humiliate or abuse others
- ❑ Sulks when he doesn't get his way
- ❑ Does not take criticism well
- ❑ Is easily hurt and insulted
- ❑ Considers most others in the world "idiots."

Extricating yourself from the grips of a narcissist who wants to keep you entrapped in many of his boxxes is complicated at best. You may or may not want to leave this relationship, however, by acknowledging and understanding it, you can decide exactly which boxxes are your own and which are not.

Be especially careful that while living with one of these individuals you don't fall into the Boxx of Guilt. They are quite good at manipulating facts, and guilt seems to be one of the easiest boxxes to get sucked into. Learn to recognize when an issue is yours and when it belongs to the narcissist. Just like the scuba diving couple, learn to recognize when feeling guilty is not a healthy way to deal with a situation.

If you do decide to get out of your narcissistic environment, you may find opportunities you never dreamed possible. One woman wrote, "I feel like I extricated myself from a cult. This type of person drives everyone around them crazy."

Before you make any decision about a narcissist in your life, do your research. One of the most in-depth books available on the subject of narcissism is called *Malignant Self-Love: Narcissism Revisited*, by Sam Vaknin, a self-proclaimed narcissist who is also highly educated in a variety of subjects. While he is not a therapist, his personal slant on this situation is very revealing and eye-opening. You can read more about his story on his website : http://smvak.tripod.com. I recommend this step to anyone who suspects they have a narcissist in their life.

Reading more details about this complicated personality may give you enough knowledge to make a decision about your relationship, or just give you tools with which to better deal with the narcissist in your life.

Whatever you do, the important thing is to realize when you have unknowingly allowed someone else's boxxes to become yours. Find new light at the end of the tunnel. The possibilities are out there!

"I feel like I extricated myself from a cult."
Survivor of a narcissistic relationship

The Investigation Leads To...

Part Four
Breaking Down The Walls

OK, so you've identified which boxxes are yours, which ones are working, and which ones you want to break down and break free of. Now what? How do you get there? Where do you start?

Keep going. You're getting close but there's still more to learn!

"Everyone has inside him a piece of good news. The good news is that you don't yet realize how great you can be! How much you can love! What you can accomplish! What your potential is!"

Anne Frank

Chapter 17
The Investigation Leads To...

My "Boxx Philosophy" came from a two-fold direction. First, the expression to "think outside the box" was becoming a recognizable phrase, although not clearly defined. Secondly, I discovered in my own journey that finding the real issues that drove me or directed my life was not an easy path. However, when I began to define and recognize my behaviors, it helped me trace my roots through my fears, and eventually back to my inner beliefs and messages. Once I uncovered those, I realized I had the power to change them. The true key was finding those deeper, ingrained beliefs I had not ever recognized before.

I'm making a big assumption that many of you may also be having a hard time finding those inner issues that are really holding you back. So my idea was to give you an easier path to follow – the path of the boxxes. By recognizing your *behaviors* (perfectionism, workaholism, and others), you can then trace your behaviors back to your fears and from there, uncover the real giant where the fears themselves were born.

I want to give you another visual analogy that might make your investigation of the boxxes more understandable and help you discover what really makes you tick. Remember, this is only my personal belief. It may work for you. It may not. You may find something else that speaks to you. The goal is to find a spark, a light bulb turning on in your head that will take you on your journey of self-discovery so that you can make your life what *you* really want it to be.

It Begins With One Drop

I live in Colorado, not far from Denver, and from my back yard I can see the Rockies looming over the entire horizon. They are magnificent and remain covered with snow long after my lawn is green and the flowers in my yard are in full bloom. As a matter of fact, it's usually not until late July before they appear to be completely barren of the last traces of snow.

As the snow and icicles begin to melt in springtime single drops form, one by one, as solid turns to liquid in the warmth of the sun. Each droplet begins its course down the mountain. As each one merges with another, they form tiny rivulets, and together they become stronger and larger. There is something they don't yet know or recognize that pulls them in a direction over which they seemingly have no control. Eventually these rivulets, with their tiny gurgling sounds, run into others like themselves and become full-fledged streams, churning and bubbling their way down the mountain. Their behavior is predictable, consistent, and fairly patterned. They begin to gather enough size to damage vulnerable areas. They are resilient and not easily deterred.

Eventually, these little streams discover that they are a part of something bigger, something even more powerful, as they dump into a vast river, a river more powerful than each individual stream, as it has the overwhelming power of many streams coming together. The sound and size are now stronger and more powerful, and its potential for damage is to be respected. If there is a flood, the river can escape its banks, tear up landscape, destroy houses, and take lives. It is feared when out of control. Yet, the river is seeking something larger still. Even though its power is vastly bigger than the small stream, it knows there is a larger power pulling it, directing it, driving its journey.

Get Out of Your Boxx

Eventually, the river discovers its mission as it pours itself into the ocean. The Mother. The Mistress of the World. Its power, when unleashed in the form of a tidal wave or tsunami, is beyond compare. It can overwhelm nations. It can kill thousands. It can cause destruction wherever it chooses. The journey of one small droplet has become a driving force with power to inflict incredible devastation.

So how does a droplet of water equate to your boxx? Look at it this way. Perhaps your perfectionistic behavior started as a child and over time this behavior escalated and became stronger, just as the stream did. (This is your Boxx of Perfectionism.) As that behavior became part of your daily ritual, it cemented its strength in your everyday life. Yet, the behavior itself didn't just happen on its own, it was a result of something bigger – the River of Fear. (You recall that all the small boxxes lead back to the Mother of all Boxxes – the Boxx of Fear.) As the river's power took over your life, it began to have some damaging results. Yet the river is not the mother – the ocean is the true culprit. Calling you. Driving you. Making decisions for you. Pulling you to do what its power demands.

What is your ocean? I believe it is self-esteem, or rather, the lack of self-esteem. Self-esteem, self-confidence, or self-image. I tie them all together and merged them into one. For simplicity sake, I will use the term Low Self-Esteem – The Ocean of Low Self-Esteem. Or in Boxx terms: The CRATE OF LOW SELF-ESTEEM! A crate that is huge and dark with shackles and huge locks on the door. It seems impenetrable. It holds you captive. It has no interest in letting you go. It is bigger than the Boxx of Fear since it permeates all of your beliefs about who you are, what you are, and where you can go in life, and it can cause horrible damage if you let it!

The Investigation Leads To...

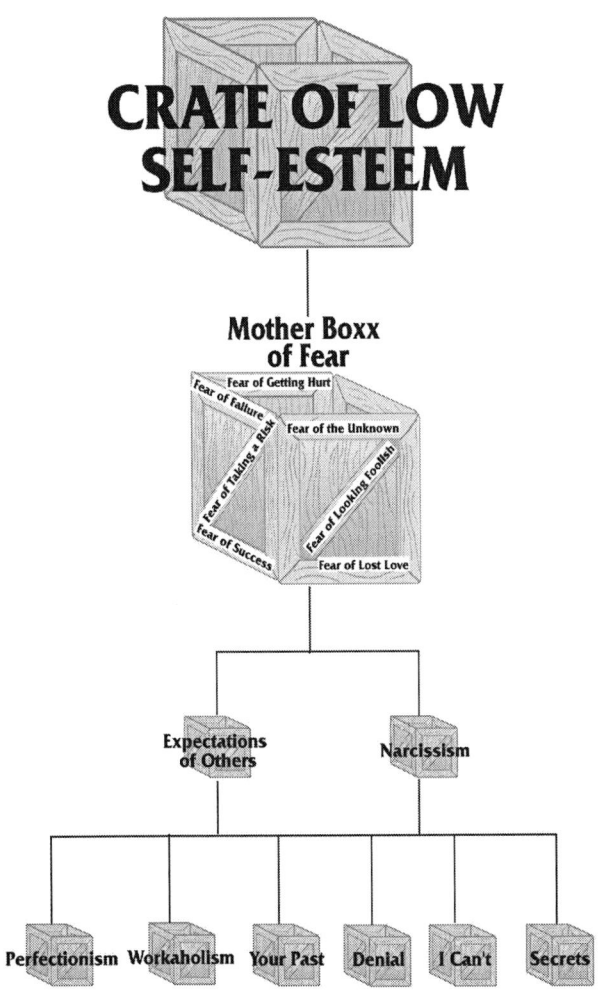

Get Out of Your Boxx

Some of the messages that are imprinted in your mind when you live in this Crate might sound like these:

- ❏ "I'm not valuable."
- ❏ "I'm worthless."
- ❏ "I don't matter."
- ❏ "I don't deserve good things."
- ❏ "Nobody loves me."
- ❏ "I'm no good."
- ❏ "I don't like myself."
- ❏ "I'm such a slob."
- ❏ "If I just weren't so stupid, ugly, short, fat ..."

These messages play in your head as a result of the overwhelming Crate of Low Self-Esteem. Until you change these inner messages and begin to build a positive self-esteem that works *for* you, the journey you are traveling will be much harder than it has to be.

Let me give you a specific example:

Let's pretend you come from a family with a perfectionist father and a shy, intimidated mother. As with most children, you seek validation and love from your parents, but somehow it's not often given. Then, one day when you are about six years old, you help Mom pick up the dinner dishes without being asked. Your father notices your behavior and praises you for your work. Bam! You found a moment of recognition and what you feel must be "love." You put that in your memory bank and try it again the next night. It works again! Your father makes a big deal about your efforts and you like the feeling. You commit yourself to picking up the dishes every night from now on.

However, after a week or so, all the fuss about how wonderful you are subsides. You can't figure it out. What changed? You decide to try something new and you get out the vacuum cleaner and vacuum the house without anyone

The Investigation Leads To...

asking you. Success! Your father thinks you walk on water again! You feel validated and "loved." You add vacuuming to your duty list and know this must be the key to believing you are a valuable person. But the same thing happens – after a while it's just an expectation that you are the one who always vacuums the house. No more fanfare. No more warm fuzzies.

So, you try another direction. You take up competitive swimming. The first time you win a meet, your father fawns all over you like you just won the Olympics! You feel vindicated! He loves you after all! You decide to win each time you compete. The feeling is too good to miss so you practice with a vengeance. If the other kids swim for 30 minutes, you practice for an hour. Every time you win, you wait for the praise, the "love." Yet, eventually, the same thing happens. Winning the local meets doesn't seem to produce the results they once did. In addition, if you come in less than first place, not only do you *not* get the praise and adoration – you get criticism. Winning second place isn't good enough – it means you are a loser. No matter how big the meet or how many competitors swam against you – even if there were 500 swimmers and you placed second — it's just another failure.

So, you practice even more. Start lifting weights to build your upper body. Start running several miles per week to strengthen your aerobic capacity. And now you participate in bigger competitions. Eventually, as you win each successive layer, the same feeling persists – the adoration and "love" are always there at the beginning, but eventually seem to fade away.

Thus, you set a new goal. The Olympics. Surely if you win the Olympics your father will love you. It will be worth a lifetime of loving. He will brag to his friends for years how you won the Olympics. And so you continue on this path and, in fact, you do win the Olympics! You proved you could do it, but not just to your father – to the world! He is so proud of you! You're on top of the world!

But guess what? The same thing happens once again. After a while, his attention wanes and his look says, "What's next?" What can you do now to show me how wonderful you are so I can I love you? So you *deserve* to be loved?"

You are devastated.

Now let's analyze this particular scenario. If you were this child, I would guess you were never given unconditional love. It was *very conditional*, as you soon found out. You were not loved for *who* you were, but for *what* you could do. You did not receive recognition, hugs, praise, or any other self-esteem builders, unless it was tied to performance. Thus, you may have built an underlying belief that said, "I am not a valuable person unless I perform." Your self-esteem became tied to performance alone. That big Crate of Low Self-esteem held you captive at a very early age. The Boxxes of Fear you fell into were Fear of Failure, Fear of Not Being Loved, Fear of the Unknown, Fear of Rejection, and perhaps many others. You began to show others your Boxxes of Perfectionism, Workaholism (where your work was your swimming career) and "I Should." Those around you may not know your self-esteem is low, low, low because on the outside you demonstrate a strong ability to work hard and always succeed in meeting your goals. You are driven. You look extremely strong. Your success in your swimming career speaks for itself. Yet, your Crate of Low Self-Esteem keeps you feeling empty, unsatisfied, unloved, and not valuable to yourself or anyone else.

Are you beginning to see the path? Does this help you start to investigate your own issues a bit deeper? Are you starting to unravel your own Crate of Low Self-Esteem and discover what might be holding you back?

While the swimmer might appear to be successful, her inner messages of being unworthy or unlovable take a toll in

The Investigation Leads To...

the three areas of her life that I mentioned earlier: her career, her relationships with others, and her health or self-care. The roadblocks she may run into may not show up for years, but they will catch up with her sooner or later. Perhaps in her career as a lawyer she may continue her perfectionistic, workaholic behaviors, eventually causing friction in her marriage. This may lead to divorce, which could, in turn, lead to depression or other physical issues. Her underlying Crate of Low Self-esteem will continue throughout her life unless she *chooses* to change it.

The good news is that she *can* change it! First, by recognizing it, and then establishing a plan using her arsenal of weapons. (You will read about these in the next chapters). To combat the situation, she must also change her inner messages and create new ones.

What would a world of High Self-Esteem look like? Well, let me share with you my visualization. First of all, it is not a boxx of any kind. It is a huge playground that goes as far as the eye can see. There are no fences around this playground. It's open and welcoming and filled with the greatest equipment — swing sets, jungle-gyms, monkey bars, teeter-totters, and three different sizes of slides. A small one, a medium one, and a *huge*, twisting, turning, waterslide type that looks scary but oh, so exciting!

Something that makes this playground unique is the surface – it's not dirt or gravel. It is more like pillows. Soft, squishy pillows. If you fall down it just bounces you back up. At the bottom of each slide and underneath the other equipment is an extra spongy pillow that first absorbs and cushions you when you fall into it, then springs you out of it so that you land on your feet again.

There is only one other highly unusual thing about this playground – it has occasional, unpredictable, severe weather. But this weather can only touch you when you are on the playground equipment, not when you are standing on the ground.

    Let's assume that I have a fair amount of self-esteem and I live in this playground. And let's say that I have a great love of plants and gardening and have decided to spend the rest of my life doing something in that business. I have been an accountant for 10 years, but have finally realized I would rather spend my day doing anything with plants and gardening than stay in accounting forever. So I get an entry-level job in a nursery and I begin to climb the small slide. Taking a job on the bottom rung at a nursery is not a huge risk other than leaving the security and benefits I received as an accountant. I spend a year learning all aspects of the nursery and garden business. My trip down this small slide holds no major risks and I reach the bottom and land in the comfort of the awaiting cushion, bouncing me up to make my next move.

    At that point I decide I want more. My Self-Esteem has been strengthened by my small success and I decide to climb the medium-sized slide by becoming the manager of the store. As I start the descent down that slide, the weather picks up and it starts to rain. I realize that the challenges I am facing as a manager are bigger and more risky. However, I have my protective Body Armor on and I know the rain is aggravating, but not life threatening. Even if it hails, as I face some bigger issues as manager, I know my armor keeps me safe and that the landing will still bounce me back on my feet, even if the hail gives me a black eye! By the time I reach the bottom of the medium-sized slide I have weathered some tough times and come out stronger because of it. I understand that while the challenges had not felt good, the end result left me more educated, wiser, and a more capable person.

    I now look to the enormous slide! It is imposing with its height and exciting design, and I know in my heart that the weather is more severe there, but the excitement of the twists and turns look so enticing! I bite the bullet and climb the many steps to the top of the slide: I decide to buy the nursery I've

The Investigation Leads To...

have been managing! I know there are financial risks. There will be business issues I may not anticipate. A war. A recession. A drought. All these issues may affect my business. But my strong Self-Esteem, which has only become stronger as I lived through the small and medium issues, leaves me ready to take on the challenge.

As I reach the top and get ready for the ride of my life, I feel the wind pick up and pull at my hair and my clothes. I take a deep breath and, believing in myself, push off on my descent. The wind attacks me, trying to blow me off, but I am not deterred. Golf-ball sized hail pelts me, but my Body Armor protects me, as I know it will. I am strong and can weather any storm because the excitement of the ride is so powerful. I know whatever the weather does to me, I will reach the bottom safely and bounce up to play again another day. Even if my nursery business turns out to be the wrong thing for me, I learn what I can, bounce up again at the bottom of the slide, and look for the next bigger slide on the playground!

NOW THAT'S STRONG SELF-ESTEEM!

A person with strong Self-Esteem doesn't get hung up in the big Boxxes of Fear. They don't get trapped in the smaller Boxxes of Perfectionism, Workaholism, Their Past, "I Can't," or any of the others. They have strong Body Armor to protect them. They make well-informed choices. They take responsibility for their actions. They use common sense. They set appropriate goals. For example, a 90-year old person doesn't set his goal to win the Boston Marathon. However, it may be completely reasonable for him to be *competing* in the Boston Marathon! (If he is in good shape, has taken care of himself, and has done the training.) People like this are not held back by Fear of Failure because they do not recognize failure as a terrible thing. They recognize it as an opportunity for growth. They do not get hung up by the Fear of "What Others Think" because they believe in themselves and doing what is right for them. They do not rely on the feedback of others to determine their self-worth. They do not fear the unknown. They believe whatever comes their way is a life lesson and that they will overcome any obstacle.

They are free.

There may not be many people with "perfect" Self-Esteem. However, I know many individuals who have a pretty strong sense of themselves. They readily admit they are not perfect. They may still weigh issues carefully. But they are on a path of their own personal freedom because they have *made* their reality. They don't believe that what life hands them is total chance. They believe in themselves. They create their own destiny.

Look around and see who you know who fits that category. Certainly on the big scale people like Oprah Winfrey come to mind. She wasn't given her life on a silver platter. She earned it. Fought for it. And was determined to win. I suspect she rarely accepts excuses or the word "NO" for an answer. She makes up her mind to do something, and she does it. Do you think luck was just handed to all the famous people in the world, or did they make it for themselves? Did John Elway get handed his career, or did he work for years to achieve it? Did Bill Gates just happen to fall into millions of dollars, or did he take some huge risks with his new ideas and run with them? Did Lucille Ball ever dream she would be a comedienne when she went to acting school and her professor told her she was a terrible actress? Or did she pick herself up and look for another slide?

OK, so we can't all be Oprah Winfrey or John Elway. But we can be the king or queen of our own small kingdom. Look around you at the people you think have "all the luck."

The Investigation Leads To...

The guy who owns three car dealerships in town. The woman who became mayor. The guy who got laid off from the technology world and now writes novels for a living. Do you think they all just "fell" into their situations, or did they *create* their lives?

Many of them may have had to battle with their boxxes, including the big Crate of Low Self-Esteem, but they mastered their fears and took the challenge. You can do the same. The next chapters will show you how.

Yet, before we move there, let me share with you one more thing. Beware. Beware of the "Army of Excuses" that will keep you from reaching your dreams. If I had let my inner beliefs that I wasn't valuable hold me back, if I had let my abusive past be my compass, if I had let the bad experiences outweigh the good ones and build my "Army of Excuses," I would not be where I am today. By focusing on the good things, I was able to find the strength that led me to take incremental risks. These risks slowly and consistently built my Self-Esteem "Playground" into one of great adventure and wonderful challenges.

You can do the same! You have the power to be whoever you want to be. Believe in yourself and take the challenge.

"It's time to stop handing random chance the power to direct your destiny. Time to make a course correction ... but it all begins with a decision not to let the faded echo of a long-ago negative event continue to shape your life. And until you make that decision, nothing will ever really change."
Mike Pilinski

Chapter 18
If Not Now, When ?

I attended a friend's funeral recently. He was only 56 years old. It seemed unbelievable to me that someone so young could be dead. As I listened to his friends speak during the service, I was overwhelmed with feelings of joy and gladness as they described how he had lived his life. He had been a commercial airline pilot but had also served his country in the military during Viet Nam, and continued in the Army Reserves for years after that. He and his wife raised a wonderful family of four great kids who had grown up and moved on with their own lives. They had been fortunate enough to travel throughout many parts of the world together, partly as a result of his career choice. When he decided to do something, he always found a way to accomplish it. He gave to others but knew how to take care of himself. I rarely saw him unhappy or heard him complain about life. And he certainly *never* knew how to be a victim. He always faced each problem that came his way and then sought a way over, around, or through it, rather than be consumed or halted by it.

When his children graduated from high school and went on to college he and his wife retired early and moved to their own private "ranch" miles from the city, complete with horses and cattle. They were thrilled with their decision and planned to spend the rest of their lives together enjoying their little slice of heaven they called "Bedlam Farm." They spent a few wonderful years living the quiet life of ranchers, enjoying some special time with each other and their animals in what seemed like their own, peaceful sanctuary. However, it wasn't long after that he began his two-year fight with cancer. That final battle was long and hard and not to be won, but during that time of introspection he realized that he had done what he wanted to do with his life. No regrets or "what if" I had done this or that. He never worried much about what others thought — he just did the right thing for himself as well as his family. He was a very lucky man with an incredibly supportive network of family and friends who brought strength as well as pleasure to his life. He certainly didn't plan on his life being cut short, but at least he had lived his time to the fullest and did what he wanted to do. He never put important things off until "someday." I left the funeral realizing just how rare a person he was.

My own father worked most of his life away. He grew up with a strong work ethic, which he instilled in my siblings and me. The downside was that he did not know how to relax. Although he loved to vacation in Florida, which meant a three-day drive in the car each way, he drove himself like a maniac just to get there. Although there were many fascinating places to visit along the way to our final destination, he could just never stop to smell the roses on the journey. Finally, one year my mother put her foot down and said she wouldn't go any more if he didn't stop to let us out and do some sight seeing periodically! He finally conceded defeat and learned to take stops here and there. It was great to see him discover some interesting tourist attractions once he slowed down long enough to notice them. I'll always remember the marine show we stopped at where a dolphin pulled me around in a little boat and my dad thought it was absolutely fascinating! Fortunately, my mom's persistence helped him to open his eyes to new things although his restlessness in slowing down the wheels of "progress" always remained a struggle for him.

In later years, my dad resisted retiring with all his might

and when he finally did stop working, he found an alternative outlet for his energy. He worked full-time for two years remodeling a house. The man just didn't know what to do if he wasn't working. Although he enjoyed puttering and creating things with his hands, by the time he finished the remodeling project, Alzheimer's disease had begun to sink its teeth in him, and the time that he and my mother could have spent traveling the world or doing other things together disappeared.

Don't misunderstand me — my father was not unhappy with his life. His work gave him a strong sense of satisfaction and fulfillment. But what great life experiences did he miss because he wasn't open-minded to trying new things and looking for the many possibilities surrounding him? What wonderful times did he and my mother miss because he didn't slow down long enough to smell the roses? He always thought there was plenty of time to do all the things he had planned for "someday" when he had time.

So the question remains, "If not now, when?" Tomorrow is guaranteed to no one. What might you be missing that could make your life better? If you don't do something that is important to you now, when will you? And furthermore, what's stopping you? When are you going to quit waiting for someday and *start taking care of you right now?*

I constantly meet people who believe in the philosophy of "*someday,* when my life is different, when I have enough time, or enough money." Yet, how often do they *make* that someday happen? How many of those "somedays" actually occur? Or how many of them slip by the wayside, as happened with my dad?

When I was trying to decide on the title of this book, I kept coming up with serious titles like "Living Out of the Boxx" or "Out of the Boxx Thinking." Things like that. Then it occurred to me that the biggest problems most people face in getting out of their boxxes are all their easy, readily available excuses. . . "I'll take care of me pretty soon, but right now I've got to drive the carpool. And by the way, since my child is only six, I'll have to do that for the next 12 years!" or, "I'm just too busy to take time for me right now — I've got 17 clients expecting me to return their calls. They have to come first!" or, "My husband wants me to make love right now and we only have five minutes, so I've got to hurry. But I promise I'll make more time for me tomorrow."

On and on and on — the excuses are always there. There's constantly something else that seems more important. You've got to clean the house, walk the dog, take Johnny to soccer practice, volunteer at school, run the PTA, do your boss a favor (hoping he'll remember you went the extra mile when it comes time for your raise), help out at church, throw a neighborhood Halloween party, get new tires on the car, go to your mother's birthday party, get your teeth cleaned, attend teacher conferences, work extra hours to help pay for the family vacation, and on and on and on and on. You are permanently stuck on the hamster wheel as long as you allow life to get in the way. Don't worry – you won't be alone. You have plenty of company. There are millions of Americans right there with you all waiting for "someday" when they have time.

When I worked in Cozumel people often looked at me curiously and asked what I was doing there. Somehow I guess a middle-aged, tall, blonde American woman sort of stood out as unusual and prompted the question on many occasions! I loved to watch their reactions when I told them my story of running away from home and escaping my treadmill to find myself. Most of them got this faraway look in their eyes and said, "Wow, you are my hero! I wish I could do that." But never in their wildest dreams did they *believe* they could do what I had done. Yet, had you asked me two years before my adventure if I would consider living and working in Mexico for six months, I would have reacted similarly. I would have thought you were insane! Or if you had asked me if I would consider starting up my own motivational seminar business I would have ruled that out as well. I never considered myself worldly enough, knowledgeable enough, or possessing enough business sense to attempt such a venture. Yet, I broke all those imaginary barriers once I got "Out of my Boxx" and finally quit waiting for "someday."

Do you believe that a lack of time and/or money is what is holding you back? Believe it or not, these are simply excuses. If a person wants something badly enough, they'll find a way! Lack of time and money give us a safe "out" for things that may seem like too much work, or too big a risk to take, even though we may "wish" for the outcome. One woman told me she couldn't possibly afford to attend a seminar for her own personal growth, but if her son needed the money for baseball she knew she would find it somehow.

I fell into the "I don't have time" trap myself for a while. I kept believing that I just didn't have time to write this book. I had too much other stuff to do getting my business off the ground. I knew that what I wanted to write was already in my head, and that it would just require a specific amount of time to get the words out on paper. However, my ongoing comments to myself and others continued to be, "I *wish* I could just lock myself up in my house for a month and do nothing else. I know I could write this book." I kept "wishing and wishing" that I could do just that, and one day I actually listened to my own seminar and hit myself over the head and said, "Quit wishing and start doing!" I knew that if I made writing the book a priority, I would make the time, and I did. Once I "found" the time, I completed the first draft within three weeks. It all came down to deciding what my priority really was, despite all my beliefs to the contrary.

I know so many people, women in particular, who put everyone in their lives first, and themselves last, in the hope that "someday" it will be their turn. I'm not saying that you should shirk your responsibilities or become so egocentric that you ignore the needs of everyone else in your life. What I am

Get Out of Your Boxx

saying is this: If you don't take care of yourself first, you're not giving your *best* you. On top of that, there's a good probability that "someday" may never happen.

In my travels speaking about living "Out of the Boxx" I meet a lot of people and am constantly amazed at their stories. One woman in her 60s was a survivor of a "Shindler's List"-type Nazi work camp, coming to this country after the war when she was still just a child. The guilt she still feels as a survivor of that ordeal when so many others died leaves her feeling responsible for taking care of everyone else in her life, but she has never felt comfortable taking care of herself. As a result, she suffers physical symptoms of stress, ulcers, heart disease and high blood pressure. Yet she keeps saying she will take care of herself "someday."

Several single mothers told me of putting their children through college and working two jobs to do so. Although they are proud of their accomplishments and the obvious love shown through these acts is evident, some of them felt a bit of resentment and anger simmering as well. The building frustration might lie underneath the surface where few will see or understand it, but the body will eventually find an outlet. Heart disease, high blood pressure, diabetes, and emotional stress – you name it, our bodies are happy to accommodate.

Of course, there are risks in life. For example, leaving your current job to try something new might seem incredibly scary and may cause you to risk losing time, energy, a change in benefits, or something else. But what if the freedom, happiness, and potential for advancement you find at another company yields greater results once you get there?

Or perhaps leaving your family to go on a week's vacation by yourself might seem "weird" to others, but maybe it's a gift that might give you time to take care of *yourself* for a change. Just think of the things your family might realize about all the things you do once you are not there to do it for them.

If Not Now, When?

You might come home and find that you are more appreciated than ever.

"If not now, when?"

I keep coming back to that question. I was so happy that my friend lived his life with that philosophy. The positive energy surrounding the people at his funeral confirmed that for me. I also say a prayer each day thanking God for showing me how to live my life this way as well. Are you ready to take a chance? Are you willing to live "Out of the Boxx?"

If Not For You, Then Who?

If you still don't feel comfortable putting yourself first maybe putting someone else you love first will still lead you to making changes. For example, Al Roker of the *Today Show* fought obesity all of his life. He tried every diet known to man. As a television personality, he was fortunate his weight had not held him back where the slim and beautiful people usually dominate the scene. He had a lovely wife and a couple of young children he adored. Yet his wife and father feared for his health. They were well aware that the health issues accompanying obesity may also lead to a shortened lifespan. Al's children could be fatherless at a young age.

While Al was equally aware of these concerns, nothing ever seemed to drive him enough to shed the weight — until he made a promise to someone who meant the world to him. Al's father, on his deathbed, begged his son to lose weight to avoid the risks of an early death. He didn't want to see his grandchildren without their father. At that moment, Al made the decision and the promise to lose the weight. After years of not making the commitment to himself, his children, or his wife, he found someone to whom his promise suddenly held more meaning.

Shortly thereafter, he set his plan into action and without telling anyone outside his immediate family, he underwent gastric bypass surgery. His success story was on television and in periodicals for weeks. He truly discovered new possibilities in his life and has improved his health considerably, but only because he made his commitment based on his promise to *someone else*.

I do not advocate gastric bypass surgery for everyone who needs to lose weight. Those decisions are best made with your doctor. However, I am suggesting that if you are having a hard time putting yourself first perhaps you can discover your power to initiate change through a back door – through someone in your life you value more than yourself.

How many women have quit drinking or smoking when they found out they were pregnant? They finally took better care of themselves, but only because they loved their unborn child more than themselves, and their commitment for change stuck.

If you are overweight and have overweight children perhaps you can find a new commitment to losing weight by putting your child's emotional and physical health first. You may remember how difficult it was growing up heavy — the teasing at school, the embarrassment changing clothes for gym class, knowing you were not popular because of your weight. By realizing that you can help give your child a better environment for building his or her self-esteem, maybe you can find new strength to attack your problems together. You can prepare healthier meals for all of you, start an exercise program, and by learning to make correct food choices, teach your kids important life skills as well. If you can't find it in your heart to lose weight for your own health issues, *do it for your kids*.

Perhaps you can quit smoking by realizing that your secondhand smoke is affecting your children's health. You can finally do it because of your love for them even if you don't feel the need to do it for yourself.

By finding your life's passion and getting off the treadmill, you can teach your children not to settle for just any job that pays the bills, but to find something that gives them fulfillment every day of their lives as well.

By believing in yourself and going back to school, even if you feel you're too old, you show your children how to be courageous, strong, determined, resilient, and open-minded — traits that will serve them well in their own lives.

By deciding to break out of your Perfectionistic Boxx, which may mean taking some risks and possibly making mistakes, you will also teach your children valuable lessons. Picking yourself up from those mistakes and trying again until you find success shows your kids that mistakes are not the end of the world, and from each mistake valuable lessons can be learned. They also learn that your love and acceptance of them as people is unchanging despite their mistakes, thus building ongoing self-esteem, which will help them in their own life challenges.

By leaving an abusive relationship and finding one where respect, kindness, trust and compassion are the foundation, you will teach your kids how to set boundaries and recognize what to look for in their own relationships.

These are all ways you can rationalize putting yourself first, if you can't seem to muster the courage to do it just for yourself. As you see, this is not egotistical — it is intelligent, realistic, and optimistic. It is just being smart.

Still having trouble deciding what your boxxes are and if you are willing to get out of them? Here are a few questions to ask yourself, including whether or not you're still waiting for someday to come along.

- ❏ Do you hate your job or feel trapped in it, but don't attempt to look for an alternative?
- ❏ Are you unhappy in a relationship but stay because it is safer, or easier than looking for a new one, or

you're afraid there isn't a better one to be found?
- ❏ Are you still supporting your children even though they are grown up, thinking that "someday" they will be able to do it on their own?
- ❏ Do you feel there is no time for *you* in your day?
- ❏ Do you keep "wishing" for things to happen but don't believe you have any control over "making" them happen yourself?
- ❏ Do you keep "hoping" that people or situations will change and someday everything will work out just fine?
- ❏ Do you use the excuse of not enough time or money to keep you from getting what you really want?
- ❏ Do you keep playing the lottery hoping that by winning, all your problems will be solved?

Above all, how are you going to feel if six months, nine months, or even 12 months from now, you are still in the same place you are today and *you haven't made any changes?*

The question remains,

"If not now, when?"

If you've finally decided now is the time to break down your boxxes then get ready because it's time for action!

"Insanity is doing the same thing over and over again, expecting a different result."
Unknown.

Chapter 19
Your Plan of Attack!

Envisioning yourself going to war with a bunch of boxxes may be a bit of a stretch of your imagination. Boxxes may not seem like dangerous enemies to you. They don't seem powerful, threatening, or to be taken seriously. It just might be a bit hard to visualize your plan of attack. So allow me to introduce something a bit more visually recognizable while at the same time a little intimidating as well! After all, if you're going to do battle, even if it's over principal, it's easier to fight an enemy you can face eye-to-eye than doing battle with an inanimate object. While a boxx may not look like a significant enemy, it could prove to be even more dangerous that coming face to face with an angry bear!

So, let's pretend again. This time you're back in the days of King Arthur's Round Table. There are knights in shining armor, damsels in distress, and there are dragons! Huge, fire-breathing, man-eating, deadly dragons! They are as big as a house and their tails alone could kill you with one blow. They appear indestructible!

Now if you were a knight in shining armor and a dragon stole your girlfriend with every intention of eating her for lunch, you would have three choices:

1) You can run headlong straight at the dragon, waving your sword and screaming at the top of your lungs without a plan of any sort, just filled with passion and a desire to win the battle!

2) You can throw up your hands and begin sobbing for the loss of your fair maiden because you know for a fact that no matter what you do, the dragon will kill you the instant you show up to save her, and you aren't suicidal.
3) You can sneak up on the dragon, take your time to carefully study his habits, and then begin to formulate a plan to save your girlfriend.

In the first scenario, charging in and attacking the dragon without a plan probably leaves you cooked from a distance, like a marshmallow over a campfire! Poof! Instant defeat. *Not* your best approach!

In the second, you just give up without trying, leaving your girlfriend to die some horrible death while you spend the rest of your life living with the guilt for not even trying to rescue her. You lose your girlfriend, your hopes, your dreams, your courage, and your self-esteem. Probably not a great option either, but it may seem safest in the short-run.

In the third option, you are the clever investigator, examining all your options and taking your time to learn who your enemy is. You observe things like what time he eats, sleeps, and goes to the bathroom. You learn how far his deadly, hot breath can reach. You may even discover where his weak spot is, for almost everyone has an Achilles' Heel. With all this information you can develop a plan. Perhaps it may be as simple as stealing your girlfriend when he leaves the cave to get his last drink of water every night before bed. Or maybe you can stab him between the eyes during his daily siesta at 2 p.m. Either way, you have studied your enemy and you know what type of plan is necessary in order to succeed — possibly without it ever even becoming life threatening at all!

My advice in attacking your boxxes is that you use the third plan. Same strategy, just different enemy. Think of your boxxes as dragons, so that you can picture your powerful and

Your Plan of Attack

dangerous enemy. See him staring you in the face, and you shooting arrows at his jugular vein, stopping him in his tracks, and watching him crumple defeated, in a giant heap! Or if you prefer the image of breaking down the walls of your boxxes with a sledge hammer, that's fine too. The important thing is to do your homework and study your boxxes in the smallest detail in an attempt to know their strengths, weaknesses, and behaviors, and with that information, determine your plan of attack.

At first, you may not feel comfortable with such personal investigation. It may be difficult to be entirely honest with yourself about things you may not want to see. Remember, what is reflected in your own mirror isn't always what you *want* to see, or *can* see. Enlisting a trusted friend whose opinion you value can help you recognize some of your more camouflaged boxxes, but remember to choose a friend you trust. Throwing the investigation open to just anyone can be lethal as it allows others who enjoy being critical to have carte blanche with your self-esteem. Either way, the more information you can uncover, the easier it will be to develop your plan. As you examine each boxx think back as far as possible (from your recent past all the way back to your childhood) to see if any of your behaviors might have a fit. Journal all the bits and pieces you uncover so you don't forget them in the overall scheme of things as your research grows.

The following is a checklist of all the Boxxes I mention within this book. It will help you begin to find your own path on your road to self-discovery. You may also come up with other Boxxes that apply only to you. Check all that might possibly apply to you, even if only on a small scale. You can prioritize them later.

Get Out of Your Boxx

Behavior Boxx Checklist

- ❏ I Can't, I Should, I Have To
- ❏ Your Past
- ❏ The Oh-So-Perfect Boxx
- ❏ Workaholism and the Wrong Career
- ❏ Weighty Boxx
- ❏ Unfulfilling Empty Boxx
- ❏ Sex Boxx
- ❏ Deadly, Secret Boxx
- ❏ Denial
- ❏ Expectations of Others
- ❏ Narcissism
- ❏ Power and Control
- ❏ Unfulfilled Relationships
- ❏ Suicidal Thoughts
- ❏ Health Issues
- ❏ Pain
- ❏ Anger/Resentment/Revenge
- ❏ Excuses
- ❏ Phobias
- ❏ Boredom
- ❏ Habits
- ❏ Impatience
- ❏ The Victim
- ❏ Unhappiness
- ❏ Pessimism
- ❏ Unlucky Me
- ❏ Poor Me
- ❏ Chronic Fatigue
- ❏ Low Expectations
- ❏ The Unloved
- ❏ Dependency
- ❏ Hate
- ❏ Jealousy

Your Plan of Attack

- ❏ Wishful Thinking
- ❏ Misunderstandings
- ❏ Resistance to Change
- ❏ Sloppiness
- ❏ Beliefs
- ❏ Sarcasm and Criticism

The Fear Boxxes

- ❏ Fear of Failure
- ❏ Fear of Success
- ❏ Fear of the Unknown
- ❏ Fear of Pain
- ❏ Fear of Being Unloved
- ❏ Fear of Being Wrong
- ❏ Fear of Taking a Risk
- ❏ Fear of Loneliness
- ❏ Fear of Loss
- ❏ Fear of Not Feeling Valuable
- ❏ Fear of Abandonment

When you've gathered as much information as you can, it's time to develop your plan. To give you an example of how to sort through all the information I thought it might help to look at all the boxxes I was locked into just prior to my Mexican leap Out Of My Boxx! As I look back on them now (and realize that I hadn't a clue what was happening to me at the time), these are the many boxxes I can identify:

Get Out of Your Boxx

Unfulfilling Relationship	Emptiness
Fear of the Unknown	Depression
Fear of Not Being Loved	Not Feeling Valuable
My Past	My Beliefs
Boredom	Claustrophobia
My Habits	Anger
Denial	The Victim

Now if I go back to being the knight in shining armor and I'm attacking a dragon with all that stuff, it can seem overwhelming! To diminish the enormity of it the next step is to define each boxx in more detail, finding where they overlap and how they rank in importance. So my investigation might reveal something like this ...

Unfulfilling Relationship

My marriage was not equally supportive or loving. I felt as though it was sapping my strength as I constantly worried about it each and every day. The stress was taking its toll on me physically and emotionally.

Emptiness

I had no feelings of direction and was getting up each day with no purpose, feeling horribly numb, as though I was in a fog. I was constantly searching for a new goal and could never find one.

Fear of the Unknown

Not knowing what might happen if I decided to file for divorce left me horribly afraid of taking the step. Would I be alone, have to sell my house, have to find a "real job"? Would I lose my horses? Would everyone hate me for my decision? Would my husband be angry at me? Would my daughter withhold her love from me because I initiated the divorce? I had so many questions here that it was overwhelming.

Depression

I slept 12 hours a day, including daily afternoon naps, and still felt exhausted most of the time. On overcast or gloomy days I needed even more sleep. I had no energy or interest in performing daily activities and found no excitement in things which I used to enjoy. I couldn't figure out why I felt so sad and bad about myself all the time.

Fear of Not Being Loved

I carried the ongoing fear that if I gave up on my marriage I might never find love again, even though my marriage didn't even feel loving at the time. I kept wondering whether an empty relationship was better than no relationship.

Anger

I had repressed and stuffed my anger for years, hoping to avoid confrontation. At times, I held it inside for so long that the least trigger would cause me to blow up, frequently resulting in screaming or throwing something. Sometimes even the dog left the room when he could sense I was about to blow.

My Past

I was tragically grieving over my past, wondering why God had let things happen to me. I felt guilty, scarred, dirty, frightened, trapped, and just plain "bad." I believed that no one could possibly understand what I was going through. And the most terrible fear of all was that the bad things from my past were *my fault* and they were destined to hang around my neck like a noose for the rest of my life.

Get Out of Your Boxx

My Beliefs

I had convinced myself that my husband was smarter, more worldly, and more important than I, and that his financial knowledge was crucial to my financial stability. I had been brought up to believe that long marriages were to be admired and that people who got divorced just didn't try hard enough. I kept trying to believe that by staying together as a family, we provided a better environment for our daughter than if we went our separate ways. And I was certain that if I filed for divorce, the world would see me as a failure.

Boredom

Without a clear direction or goal, I wandered around aimlessly, doing the same thing, day after day, never finding anything new or exciting in my life.

Claustrophobia

My memories of the abuse led me to being fearful of ever being trapped again. Whenever I felt pinned in, my habit was to run away, whether that be physically trapped, emotionally confined, or even just finding myself in small spaces filled with people. My automatic reaction was to flee. I frequently had to get in my car and leave the house when I felt too much emotional turmoil. This behavior left my family feeling abandoned and extremely frustrated.

My Habits

I fell into the habit of taking a nap every afternoon, doing routine, mundane chores (which provided mindless activity) and burying myself in carpool duties, feeding the animals, and anything else which could provide me a sense of stability at a very unstable time.

Denial

I kept denying that things were engulfing me. While I recognized some of my boxxes, there were many I did not. In addition, I kept "hoping" that many of them would just get better over time. I saw a therapist weekly, and although she provided some relief and guidance, my underlying issues still controlled me.

The Victim

It was easy to fall into the mindset of "poor me" and not take responsibility for my situation. It gave me an excuse for all my actions, or inactions, and laid blame on someone else, or simply blamed fate or luck. It gave me permission not to do anything to rectify the situation.

Low Self-Esteem

I lived with a constant emptiness inside – a feeling that no one needed me — that my existence was meaningless. That no matter what I did, it wasn't good enough. Because of that, I felt as though I may as well quit trying to do anything. Apparently I didn't do anything right to begin with, so maybe it was safer not to do anything at all. I kept expecting to find my inner validation through the external praise of others and that ongoing mission only continued to lead me to disappointment.

Keep in mind that I was at an all-time low at that moment in my life. If your list of boxxes isn't this big, you're in a much better place to begin with. The other good news is that making changes when you're in a position of searching for answers, but not being desperate for them, gives you much more clarity in your vision and perhaps can make it easier to create change. However, if you are in as many boxxes as I was, do not despair! Our next step is how to figure out your best plan of attacking your boxxes, no matter how few or how many you've identified. Don't forget that some of the boxxes can still be protective as well, so don't rule them all out as you analyze them.

OK, so you have done your research and have made your lists of detailed and specific feelings and issues you've uncovered. Your next step is to scale down the huge pile into a workable one by setting priorities and checking for any overlapping issues. Here's how I would sort mine out:

First, my dominant boxxes were Unfulfilled Relationship and Emptiness. These also tied directly into Depression, Boredom, and Habits.

Second, the issues of abuse which haunted me from my past had taken over my life. My self-image and self-esteem were tied to my Victim Boxx and left me feeling unable to control my destiny. My Claustrophobia Boxx provided some safety and helped me recognize that when it came time for fight or flight, flight was my safest option. My deep-seated Boxx of Anger, buried for years, was screaming to get out and as I had ignored it for so long, it was a festering, lethal, suffocating boxx that tainted many areas of my life.

Third, my Boxxes of Fears of the Unknown and Not Being Loved kept me paralyzed, unable to move or make any decisions. This kept me on the treadmill day after day with no hope for relief in sight. My Belief Boxx, concerning issues of love and marriage, was based upon the Expectations of Others. My Denial Boxx kept my head buried in the sand like an ostrich, hoping that "someday" when I finally had the courage I would pull my head out and everything would be magically changed into the fantasy world that I dreamed of.

The underlying issue, of course, was that my Crate of Low Self-Esteem was enormous! Who was I? What drove me? What did I love doing more than anything? How could I find validation from within myself instead of requiring it from those around me? Who was I to think I deserved better to begin with?

Your Plan of Attack

My plan, as it turned out, was quite unconscious. It was based purely on survival. It looked something like this:

- ❏ My protective Boxx of Claustrophobia kept me safe and told me to run as far away as I could; that to heal, I needed space, time and solitude.
- ❏ I found myself seeking to know what was truly important to me. Who was I without all the material and personal things that defined me?
- ❏ I recognized that I had to change some of my beliefs about love and marriage, My Past, and the Expectations of Others.
- ❏ I had to face my fears because they were paralyzing me and restricting every aspect of my behavior, my thoughts, and my life.
- ❏ I had to take better care of my body, my mind, and my spirit.

This is only one example of how separating your behaviors into more recognizable boxxes can help give you a roadmap for where you want to go. Let's look at a less complex combination of boxxes for another person.

We met George in Chapter 7. He is the guy who has to vacuum his carpet every day. As he broke down his boxxes they looked like this:

Perfectionism

George has an inner feeling that drives him to keep his house and work environment spotless. He experiences an extremely unsettling and restless feeling if these things are not done. He recognizes that there is a fine line between being clean and being compulsively neat, and realizes that he falls into the latter category. He is confused about why anyone would think this behavior might have any negative connotations, yet his friends and loved ones constantly tease him

Get Out of Your Boxx

about his rituals.

Routines and Habits

He finds comfort in doing things the exact same way every day and doesn't understand why he becomes uncomfortable when presented with any unanticipated surprise, either good or bad.

Resistant to Change

He is painfully slow to try new things and is frustrated when people want him to do so when the old ways still work just fine.

Fear of Failure

He has an overriding Boxx of Fear of Failure, especially for things he has never before attempted. Thus, he finds it better to stay with the tried-and-true methods than to risk new ones which might risk failure.

Fear of Not Being Loved

George fears that if he fails, he will not be loved by those around him. This underlying fear is what drives him to overachieve and not risk making any mistakes.

Confusion

He doesn't understand why his routines and behaviors should bother or affect anyone else.

Self-Esteem

George's self-esteem is tied to his performance and not to his belief in himself as a person. Fortunately, he is an intelligent, sensitive, caring man who always seeks opportunities for self-improvement. As he studied his boxxes he developed the

Your Plan of Attack

following overall understanding:

Summary

His Crate of Low Self-Esteem is all encompassing and has been so throughout his lifetime. He believes that *who* he is, is 100 percent based upon *what* he does and *how well* he does it. As a result, he is constantly setting himself extremely high standards, and his overwhelming fear is that he may not be able to meet those standards. By staying within his safety zone of routines and habits and avoiding new things, he avoids taking on any new risks that could lead to failure. While this strategy feels safe, the comments he receives from others lead to confusion about his perfect performance, which they do not find as rewarding as he hopes. He would like to resolve his confusion and feel less pressure in his life.

George's plan, based upon this information, might be something like this:

- ❏ Find ways to build self-esteem.
- ❏ Learn to take risks that may intentionally lead to small failures.
- ❏ Assess whether others still love him in spite of these small failures.

From here, he needs to decide which steps might best help him achieve these directions. His first choice was whether to take Baby Steps or Giant Leaps to achieve his optimum results.

Baby Steps Or A Giant Leap?

OK, so you have done your homework and your research has revealed some obvious patterns of behavior that point to the most visible path towards uncovering your

Get Out of Your Boxx

boxxes. What's the next step?

First of all, it is important to remember that all the boxxes lead back to the all-encompassing Boxx of Fear, and that no matter what steps you attempt, there will probably be some fear involved! But on the positive side, if you also realize that fear is there, whether you take these steps or not, you can make your commitment to change a little easier!

For some of you, starting with Baby-Step changes will be your safest move. For others, taking a Giant Leap Out of Your Boxx may be the only way you will ever change. In my case, I was at one of those crisis moments in my life where I knew that if I didn't change something in a big way that I would just find myself right back on that treadmill again, and that was a bigger fear than taking an enormous risk.

George decided to start by taking Baby Steps. He began by promising himself he would not vacuum the carpet on Mondays or Fridays. To help keep him on task, he circled those two days on the calendar each week and made a check mark on each day he remained committed to his promise. As this became a new part of his routine and he found his friends and family still loved him just the same, he began to think about making other small changes. As he builds his self-confidence, bit by bit, he may even work up to taking a bigger risk. A Giant Leap for George might be to leave his dishes in the sink overnight, one night per month! While this may seem miniscule to most of us, it may seem overwhelming to him at the beginning, but by realizing that he has only committed to one day a month he can still cling to the knowledge that his safe routines are ever-present. In the overall scheme of things, he will hopefully recognize that his world has not fallen apart due to these changes. This knowledge may lead him to feel more comfortable continuing on his journey of new possibilities. In the process, he may even free up more time to spend with his loved ones! A long term Giant Leap for George might be to plan a vacation outside of his usual comfort zone.

Your Plan of Attack

Baby Steps

The following are ideas that may help you think of some Baby Steps that might work for you:

- ❏ Try out a new hairstyle. Even something as simple as changing which side you part your hair on might be a fun way to start. One of our recent presidents did just that and it was in the news for days!
- ❏ Instead of jumping into another diet, simply write down everything you eat every day for a month. You don't have to change anything you eat whatsoever, you only need to make the promise to record it – accurately! This step may give you an enormous amount of knowledge concerning your current nutrition and caloric intake. With this in mind, you may decide to take further steps later.
- ❏ Change your attitude in a small way. When someone asks you how you are, always reply with "I'm wonderful!" (The secondary benefit to this is that you may improve the attitudes of those around you as well, and they may not offer you their "tales of woe" when you ask about them!)
- ❏ Start a success log. This does not have to be a typical diary or journal where you write about absolutely everything that happened that day. Just record something each day that gave you success. Maybe someone paid you a complement, you did something nice for a neighbor, you finished a project at work, or even something as simple as giving yourself a pat on the back for smiling all day! When you look back over your success log after a month, it will give you a way to remember the many positive things you achieved over time and not just concentrate on the negative ones.

- ❏ Buy an item of clothing you might never choose for yourself. And to make it even better, choose a color you wouldn't normally wear and see if anyone notices.
- ❏ Pick up a personal-growth tape or book at your library and see what other ideas you can glean. There are so many wonderful people who can get you motivated. Listen to as many of them as you can, because each person has a different slant or may say something in a slightly different way that speaks to you. Some of my personal favorites are Oprah Winfrey, Dr. Phil McGraw, Anthony Robbins, and Brian Tracey, to name but a few. Even if you only get one "spark" from each of them, after a while all those sparks might create a bonfire in you!
- ❏ If you've never tried it, go to a movie alone. It can be a great way to try out small steps of independence.
- ❏ Promise yourself that for 30 minutes one night a week you get to soak in the tub without *ANY* interruptions. Announce this plan to your family so they don't bother you with phone calls, requests for homework help, or anything else. Make it *your time* and take care of *you* first!
- ❏ Schedule a massage – you deserve it!
- ❏ Ask your neighbor if she wants to swap cooking for a night. Since it's so easy to get tired of making your favorite recipes, you make one of your favorites and she'll make hers. Then, you swap the finished product and get to eat something new without the headaches and risks of trying out a new recipe yourself.
- ❏ Make a mental note each time you use the phrase "I can't" and change it to "I don't *choose* to."
- ❏ Block every Friday night off on your calendar for Family Time and nothing else. Write it in ink in big

Your Plan of Attack

red letters for a month and try it out.
- ❏ Instead of immediately saying no to a new opportunity, start saying yes! Ask yourself what you really risk if you try it and fail.
- ❏ Change your wording from "I don't have time" to "It's not my priority right now." Even if you don't feel comfortable saying it aloud to other members of your family at the beginning, start by saying it to yourself.
- ❏ Establish new boundaries and say "*NO*" to something small that everyone always expects you to do.
- ❏ Buy something small once a week just for you.
- ❏ Try out a new restaurant you haven't been to before.
- ❏ Do the same things you usually do in a typical day but change the order in which you do them.
- ❏ Study the classified ads for jobs in your paper each week. Call as many as might fit your interests and get as many details as possible regarding the job. You never know what you might discover!
- ❏ Try something absolutely different like Belly Dancing! It sure looks like fun and might slim your waist, increase your energy, and liven up your sex life!

Giant Leaps

After you've had success with a number of Baby Steps (or if you're just ready to leap now), you might try some of these Giant Leaps!

- ❏ Go back to school at night or online.
- ❏ Quit your job (if it's fiscally responsible to do so) and start your own business. Do your research first so you set yourself up for your best probability of success.
- ❏ Move to another part of the country or the world.

(Again, do your homework ahead of time so you know what you'll find when you get there.)
- ❏ Make time for something that has always been an interest in your life but you never got around to making a priority. Write that book you've always wanted to write. Submit your photography to *National Geographic!* Design your own house.
- ❏ Take up a new sport or hobby. Explore scuba diving, polo, bridge, fencing, or karate!
- ❏ Make a commitment to lose weight and jump in with both feet!
- ❏ Try something like hypnosis, acupuncture, light therapy, or other alternative self-care treatment.
- ❏ Recommit yourself to your relationship 100 percent and take steps to improve it. Don't just keep waiting for it to improve by itself or –
- ❏ Leave an unfulfilling relationship and search for a more rewarding one.
- ❏ Set appropriate boundaries for your teenagers and stick with the punishments you dish out.
- ❏ Set boundaries that make you feel safer and fulfilled in your sex life.
- ❏ Plan a totally different vacation this year. Maybe even go without your family! Make it *your* time and give them *theirs!*
- ❏ Say *NO* to some big thing someone always just expects you will do. Furthermore, don't give them some lame reason why you're backing out. Be honest and let them know that you need to spend some quality time on *you* first!
- ❏ If you're afraid of heights, stare it in the face and try parasailing or hot air ballooning with someone you trust.
- ❏ If you have been in bad relationships and have been hurt, remind yourself how you kept getting your

Your Plan of Attack

knees banged up when you first learned to walk, and just get back out there and try dating again!
- ❏ Go ahead and ask your boss for the raise you feel you deserve!
- ❏ Tell your grown children that it's time for them to pay their own way. If they have a job but are still living in your house, discuss a room and board arrangement and teach them to be accountable and responsible.
- ❏ Have a family meeting to discuss various options to help spread the workload around. There's nothing that says boys can't do the laundry or the vacuuming. Don't take on all the traditionally female jobs as yours just because you're a woman, or vice versa.

These ideas should get you started on your journey. Remember, whether you take Baby Steps or Giant Leaps to get Out of Your Boxx, you must use common sense, be safe, not destroy other people's boundaries, or break any laws. Leaving young children alone at night while you go to night school is not responsible. Neither is fasting for two weeks to lose weight because you think it might be the only way to win your battle with your weight. Once again, seek input from your friends or family. Just remember there are many saboteurs on your journey as well. (We'll deal with them in Chapter 20!)

Be true to *you!* Take care of *you!* Be honest with yourself. Be careful. Try new things. And look for the possibilities surrounding you!

"Determine that the thing shall be done, and then we shall find the way."
Abraham Lincoln

Chapter 20
Your Powerful Weapons

*B*efore you begin to break down your boxxes, it's important to know which weapons you have in your arsenal. A good warrior not only knows what tools he has available, but how to use them. In addition, he is well-versed in what tragedies may occur if he uses his weapons inappropriately or carelessly. Not only might he fail at his mission, he can hurt himself or others in the process.

You have three very potent weapons at your disposal:

1) The Words you use
2) The Commitments you make
3) The Visualizations you create

Words

Words can be as powerful as any nuclear warhead. They may be incredibly useful when used as a threat, or can easily annihilate enemies if released. However, if they are used inappropriately or for the wrong reason, they can unleash devastation, and like nuclear fallout traveling far beyond its original destination, can leave pain and despair everywhere.

You may already be suffering from scars left by the power of words used during various times in your life. Try these memories on for size:

❏ "You are such a loser. I can't believe you are my

child."
- ❏ "You are too fat to wear a bikini."
- ❏ "Can't you do anything right?"
- ❏ "I wish you were never born."
- ❏ "You are so stupid."
- ❏ "You're such a klutz."
- ❏ "You're not smart – you're just the teacher's pet."
- ❏ "Quit being a crybaby – be a man."
- ❏ "You made a mess of this again?"
- ❏ "You have the ugliest nose on the planet."
- ❏ "You are just plain selfish."
- ❏ "You are very bad!'
- ❏ "You haven't got a lick of common sense."
- ❏ "Why can't you be more responsible?"

Are you starting to believe in the power of words yet? I'll bet that everyone remembers certain words that sting even years after they were first uttered by whoever used them as weapons. The word "selfish" has a particularly nauseating response to me whenever I hear it.

Using words as weapons can be intentional or unintentional. Take teasing, for example. While direct, critical teasing is obviously deadly, there is a subtle kind of teasing that seems to be well-meaning and lighthearted but still carries heavy underlying messages, whether aimed at others or yourself. Your subconscious has a tendency to pick up those subtle messages, even if your conscious self doesn't. In fact, many would argue that even good-natured teasing has a hint of truth to it.

For example, my friend Joy was at the grocery store one day when the clerk asked where she had found her cute, young daughter who had accompanied her shopping. Although she loved her child more than life itself and would have never intentionally hurt her in any way her response, which was meant to be humorous, could have been taken the wrong way under certain situations. She told the clerk, "Oh, I

Your Powerful Weapons

just found her lying out in the street with the trash." If children hear these messages, over time they may start to believe they are no better than trash. Thus, the slow erosion of self-esteem begins, sadly brought on by a well-meaning parent who had no idea that something said in fun could lead to a negative result.

Another example is how we sometimes joke about ourselves. Again, not meant to be hurtful, but offered as humor and sometimes to break the tension in an uncomfortable or unfamiliar situation. Take my web designer, for instance. She had only created three other websites before designing mine. Yet, when I stopped by her house to get the first "sneak peak," I couldn't believe the incredible work she had done. It was fabulous! She was creative, incorporated music on each page, and had demonstrated an excellent feel for layout and use of photos. Her work left me speechless! As I was about to leave, her husband walked in the door and she announced, "Well, she's not going to fire me. At least she didn't hate it!"

This was all said in humor and with no condescension, but the underlying message she was giving herself was that her work really wasn't *that* great when, to the contrary, it was magnificent! She didn't need anyone else to chip away at her self-esteem – she was doing a thorough enough job all by herself!

I explained that by using her own words as a source of power to help her build her confidence (and her business!) she could have substituted words such as these to strengthen her armor, "Wow, she was so excited about my work and the website, I am thrilled to death. She loved my ideas, the music, the layout — everything. I feel like I walk on water!"

These are messages you can give yourself and those around you each and every day as you do battle to get Out of Your Boxx. The more self-confidence and self-esteem you can build for yourself, the easier your mission becomes. Fighting that great big Boxx of Fear isn't so hard when you believe in yourself, and that's where words give you power! It is empowering to realize that if you can be "brainwashed" with negative messages, you have the power to reverse those old messages and replace them with new ones – a "positive brainwashing!"

These simple weapons are free, are always at your disposal, and are not difficult to use. However, learning to use them takes some training. It's always easier to fall back into old habits of tossing words around as though they are meaningless. But with some direction and persistence you can learn to use words that empower you to start a mission to destroy your boxxes!

Try substituting old brainwashing statements with these wonderful, positive weapons that can be used in your favor:

- "I am a smart, educated, positive person."
- "I am energetic and optimistic."
- "I can do anything I put my mind to."
- "I determine my destiny. Luck has nothing to do with it."
- "I find success in everything I do."
- "I enjoy challenges."
- "I always make healthy choices for myself and my family."
- "I make time for things that are important in my life."
- "I love my child unconditionally."
- "Roadblocks don't stop me. I just learn to go around them."

These are examples of how words can give you back your power if you make a conscious effort in putting them to use *for* you. By being careful with the words you use, you can direct yourself and those around you on a path towards positive results. The hardest part may be educating your friends and family members to use *their* words to help you in your quest for self-improvement. In fact, they may help themselves along the way as well.

Consider two conversations I had with my group of women friends I have lunch with nearly every week. In the first example, I was sharing with my friend, Sue, how I was in a wonderful new relationship with a man I had met and worked with in Mexico. I was very excited about the relationship and the possibilities of what the future might hold for us. As she listened to me, she responded with all intentions of being a caring and supportive friend, but her choice of words could have easily sent me the wrong message. She said, "Well, Mary Jo, I just hope he doesn't hurt you." Of course, what she meant was that she hoped I would not get emotionally hurt by the relationship, and that it would turn out the way I wished it to. What my brain *could* have heard and held on to was, "Be careful. Men almost always hurt women in some way. Don't take any unnecessary risks." Had my self-esteem been at a low point, those words could have carried much more negative power.

Understanding the power of words, I told Sue what her message could have created in my mind had I let it, and suggested that by changing her words to, "I hope this is the greatest relationship of your life," I was more directed towards strength and optimism in my relationship. I subconsciously set a path to do things which could make the relationship grow, instead of anticipating it failing and helping it to do so.

The second situation, within the same group, occurred when Sue was extremely sad and depressed over a difficult situation in her life. Our group was very supportive and offered our shoulders to cry on and our ears to listen. However, one of the other women named Jane remarked to Sue, "Be sure to take your time recovering, Sue. Depression isn't easy to get rid of and I'm sure it will take you some time to feel better."

Now on the surface this seems like a comforting, understanding, very caring statement, and was truly meant with all those intentions. Yet, these fairly harmless words instructed Sue subconsciously that no matter what she might want or think, she was going to be suffering from depression for some time to come. In other words, it gave Sue permission to stay in her boxx and not do anything proactive to get out. It also let her become a victim of circumstance, thus taking away her power.

Worded in a more positive, powerful way, Jane could have given Sue some tools to help her out of her boxx by saying, "Sue, I know you feel bad right now. You've just experienced some tough things and I know how much that can hurt, but I also know what a strong woman you are. You have overcome so many difficult situations in the past. You are truly a survivor. We're here to help you get your strength back however we can, so that you can get back on track as soon as possible!"

Which would you rather hear and which do you think might help Sue recharge the fastest?

Here are some other key words to be careful with in your day-to-day communication with yourself:

"I wish ..."
"I hope..."
"I'll try ..."

Wishing, hoping, and trying all imply that you do not have control over your life or your decisions – that you are waiting for someone to wave a magic wand over you and produce results you do not have to work for. "Wishing" to win the lottery because it would solve all financial problems has proven untrue for many winners. If they were poor money managers before they won a fortune, they remain so, and frequently are bankrupt quickly. Instead of "wishing" good things would fall into their laps, they would fare better by devising a good budget and sticking to it. Instead, they stay in their

Boxxes of Wishful Thinking and continue with the behaviors that got them into trouble to begin with.

"Hoping" that "someday" you will lose weight because you think your life will be different blames your situation on pure luck. It allows you to feel comfortable as a victim and gives you permission not to take responsibility for your choices.

"Trying" to do something implies that you aren't fully invested in the activity to begin with. If someone says they'll "try" to come to your birthday party, do you count on them to be there, or give them a 50-50 chance of showing up? If you "try" to quit smoking, then you don't really believe it's possible to begin with.

Change those three wishy-washy statements to these:

"I DO make wise financial decisions."
"I AM making healthy changes in my eating patterns."
"I MADE THE DECISION to quit smoking."

These statements are proactive and demonstrate that you are taking action and responsibility for your behaviors. When you can do that, you give yourself power and freedom over the possibilities in your life and you refuse to take on the role of the victim or one who sits on the sidelines.

I have also used my words differently to plan for a different outcome surrounding the word "fight." We all assume that we'll have fights with our friends or loved ones from time to time, right? My friend J.J. told me that on his wedding day his father turned to him and said, "My son, I'm glad you're happy today, but just keep in mind that not every day will be like this. Some days you'll have some rip roaring fights." Of course, people are human and not always in agreement, so his father's words were not uncommon or meant to be insulting or condescending. However, what they did do was *predict* that "rip roaring fights" would be in his son's future.

Get Out of Your Boxx

To begin with, I take particular offense to the word "fight" in relationships. Any type of fight implies that someone wins and someone has to lose. I spent too many years on the losing end of fights as my ability to argue logically has never been my strongest asset. Thus, I have chosen to replace the word "fight" with "Learning Opportunity." If I run across an opportunity where I can learn something that will benefit me in the long run, then that is a positive thing in my opinion. So, if I only allow "learning opportunities" in my relationships, I am more willing to confront a problem because I already believe I will learn something from the situation and will know how to handle it better the next time. In addition, I am not assuming that one party has to win and the other one lose. With communications based upon unconditional love and/or respect (depending on whether it is an intimate relationship or not), each person should feel their opinions are heard and valued, despite the final outcome.

Think of other re-wordings you might use for your specific situations. Remember to choose your words wisely and carefully. Slow your conversation down to give yourself as much time as possible to make the best word choice for each situation. Words are ready ammunition so use them carefully for yourself and those around you.

Commitments or Intentions

Another strong weapon is your Level of Commitment or Intention on reaching your goals. These words describe your belief that you are truly able to accomplish something, once you put your mind to it. It doesn't really matter what you call it, as long as you understand the idea. It all comes down to just how dedicated you are to making change happen.

Looking back in time there are countless examples of people who gave of themselves 100 percent to something they wanted to achieve. Motivational speakers throughout the world tell the story of Thomas Edison and his quest to invent the light bulb. Edison's friends must have thought he was completely crazy. Despite hundreds and hundreds of experiments that failed, he persevered towards his goal. He must have known about the power of words, for he is reported to have told a colleague, "I haven't had a thousand failures, I have discovered a thousand ways *not* to invent a light bulb." That man had an unfailing commitment and, as such, realized his dream.

President John F. Kennedy was committed to getting a man on the moon. He didn't know how to do it. He just knew that by making that commitment to the American people, he was already halfway there, and the mission was eventually accomplished. He never once said, "We'll try." He said, "We will." And he meant it. He had *no intention* of accepting anything less.

When we look at superhuman feats of strength, willpower, or engineering, they all come down to the fact that the people behind them demonstrated 100 percent Intention or Commitment towards reaching their goals. Many times people don't even know *how* they will accomplish something when they first set out to attain it – they just first become committed to the results.

Let's consider the situation where you finally decide to quit smoking. You just found out you're pregnant and you want a healthy baby more than anything. So you decide it's time you quit. Period. No excuses. You make a promise to yourself that you are *100 percent Committed* to the plan. At this point, do you think it matters what path you choose in your smoking cessation program? Will it matter if you use a nicotine patch, quit cold turkey, or undergo hypnosis? *No!* Whatever method you choose will work *if you are 100 percent Committed to the outcome!*. If your Intention is 100 percent — not 50, 75, or even 95. If it's not 100 percent, *then don't waste your time to begin with!*

For many of us, it becomes so easy to fall into the

"good enough" philosophy. Let's say it sounded like a good idea to quit smoking for the baby, but when those cravings start showing up, you rationalize that smoking isn't really *that* bad for children. After all, they're not inhaling. You suddenly justify that maybe you'll *cut down* your consumption, not stop completely. Surely, that will be "good enough." You won't have to work so hard to quit all the way, but by cutting back you'll still be doing your child a favor. Right? Yet you will be doing your child no favor if you eventually get lung cancer and die. What happened to your level of Commitment?

Here is where you have to do some strong inner soul searching. Let's use the weight-loss example again. *What really is your commitment to losing weight?* If it's your 100 percent Intention to lose, then it won't matter what method you use — Weight Watchers, the Atkins Diet, Cabbage Soup Diet, counting calories, or becoming a marathon runner. However, if in your soul you don't feel you deserve to be thin, or that you are safer from sexual advances when you are heavier, or people won't expect certain things from you if you are overweight, or you are genetically stuck with your weight, or whatever your reason that weight loss is impossible for you, THEN DON'T GO ON ANOTHER DIET! You will only be disappointed with the results once again, and probably end up blaming the diet.

However, you have the ability to alter your intention! This is where examining your boxxes can determine which fears are really holding you back. Find your issues. Identify them. Study them. See a counselor, coach, or hypnotist to help you uncover issues you can't find on your own. Do something different to get Out of Your Boxx and make the changes you keep dreaming about!

If you can't find enough reason within yourself, then find an external reason to lead you to 100 percent Commitment. Take charge of your weight and your food habits because you want to do it for your children's sake. Teach them good eating habits before they grow up facing pressures confronting overweight children. Do it *before* your doctor starts talking about diabetes and insulin injections. Do it because *you are a valuable person* and can do whatever you set your mind to! Nike's slogan says it all, *"JUST DO IT!"*

With 100 percent Intention you can move mountains. It has brought us feats of engineering that are centuries old. It can start wars, end wars, and save lives. It has changed people's lives. *IT CAN CHANGE YOURS!* Just know how to use it in your weapon arsenal, and don't go into any battle without it.

Visualization

Think of Visualization as another one of those methods to reverse negative brainwashing and make it your power tool to create new positive brainwashing! Visualizing what you want is not new or uncommon. However, some people may not realize that it is indeed a weapon of fierce power. Instead of using detailed visualizations, they sort of have a vague idea of what their goals look like. They may even cut out photos of a slim woman to put on their refrigerator as a reminder of exactly what they want to look like at the end of their diet. Or maybe if their goal is to get a promotion to management they have a picture of someone in a business suit speaking to a board room full of people. They stare at that photo every day with their face superimposed upon the body of the person wearing the suit. Yet the visualization I'm talking about is so much more than that. It involves incredible details, is practiced daily, and needs to be planned out with strategy and foresight.

Have you ever tried to make a cake without a recipe, or without knowing what flour or eggs looked like, or how to use a mixer? Or, how about the many great builders of the world – did they just throw their building together without an architectural plan? Of course not. They knew exactly what their bridge or building would cost to build, what color it would be,

Get Out of Your Boxx

how much time it would take to build, had drawings of the specific steps in the building process, knew how many people and what equipment were required in each step, and finally, could see each beautiful detail of their project when it was completed! All of these details were imbedded in the mind's eye of the person creating the project even before the first shovel of dirt was dug.

Do you have this kind of visualization about what you want things to look like once you break out of your boxxes? It might be a new, thinner you. Or a new invention you're going to design. Or can you see yourself in a loving, caring relationship? Well how are you supposed to know how to reach your goals if you don't have in your mind exactly what all the items look like in the development of your plan?

It's time to help you develop your own "life movie" or visualization. First of all, get yourself paper and pencil and think of all the details you want to see in your movie. Most importantly, start with the end result you are seeking. We'll backtrack with other pieces of the puzzle from there.

I'll get you started by using my own visualization. When I started my *Out of the Boxx* business my goal was to facilitate week-long seminars in Cozumel every month. So, I started with exactly what my graduation ceremony was going to look like. To me, this represented the culmination of the week's activities in one grand, final moment. Since I had worked at the hotel where the seminar was going to be held, I was able to recreate the environment down to the smallest detail. I picture the auditorium with the lights dim, the participants carrying small candles as they walk down the carpet-lined aisle to take their seats. The music playing as they enter is from the original Rocky movie (I'll explain how I use Rocky later), and I am standing on the stage, smiling at all the successful participants who exude happiness, excitement, and new confidence from their successful week of introspection and relaxation.

Your Powerful Weapons

I know exactly what outfit, earrings, and other jewelry I am wearing. I also picture my body, which has become rock-hard from all the exercising I have been doing to get in shape for this moment. My abdominal muscles are defined, my stomach flat, my skin tanned. I am filled with overwhelming satisfaction that my dream has become a reality. I even have my speech for this ceremony planned in detail. I see myself inviting each graduate to the stage to receive their diploma and a single rose, and listening to each one talk about what the week meant to them. After the graduation ceremonies finish, the entire group has a wonderful party in the disco, celebrating in style! I also picture the financial results from my seminar, and see the amount on the check I deposit in the bank upon my return from the seminar. (There needs to be a practical side to my visualization as well.)

OK, so that is step one. I see all the details of the end result. In my next step I work backwards and fill in even more details. I envision what my group looks like as they get off the plane, as they arrive at the hotel, as they form new friendships and discover the wonders of the island and the "Out of the Boxx" activities and experiences.

From there I go back even further and see the work I do at home prior to arriving at the seminar. I see myself talking to various groups, writing my columns, doing radio appearances, and anything else to market my business. Now I'm ready to put all these things in a specific order as my success movie. I list everything I want in my visualization in as much detail as possible. The more details, the better.

The final step is to find a quiet place each day to "watch" your life movie in your mind. It may be when you first wake up in the morning and lie quietly in bed for an extra 30 minutes safely snuggled under your warm covers. Or perhaps your household is noisy and too busy in the morning and you need to wait until late at night when it slows down to find a quiet corner in your study to claim as yours. For me, my hot tub calls and I soak at the end of each day, without music, interruption, or sunlight to distract me. It is *my* time and I give it to myself.

I allow about 30 minutes to go through my entire visualization, beginning first with relaxation techniques to quiet my mind. Start with slow, deep breathing to calm your brain and body so that you can be the most receptive to the messages you are trying to plant. You may choose to lie down, recline, sit up – it doesn't matter, as long as you are comfortable and don't fall asleep in the process! Think about all of your muscles turning to jelly as you give yourself permission to leave the outside world and all the accompanying stresses behind you. Close your eyes and begin your movie.

In my movie I spend most of my time on the final scene. I feel the excitement, elation, and satisfaction of my success in sharing my message with others. Since my need to help other is always one of my foundation beliefs, this feeling gives me power as well as direction, for I know I will be successful in my mission as long as I stay the course. After I am firmly entrenched in the final scene, I slowly rewind and review the steps I took to get to that final scene. This important piece shows you exactly what you have to do to get there: place phone calls, prepare reports, or in the case of weight loss, write down what you eat every day. It is your roadmap for all those little steps you need to do to become successful.

Now here's my silent weapon: I build two doors into my visualization. One says "IN" and the other says "OUT." The IN door allows room for additional possibilities to enter my life that I may not have thought about in developing my movie. For example, my original visualization did not address writing a book at any early stage whatsoever. Yet, when that idea suddenly seemed vastly important, I allowed it in my "Possibility Door – the IN door."

The "OUT" door is quite the opposite. How many times do you catch yourself listening to that little negative voice in your head? You know – the one that is constantly telling you that you're not good enough, smart enough, or that you're never going to make a living doing what you love? You will be replacing those bad thoughts with good ones as you master the power of words; but in the meantime, that nasty voice can sometimes be quite persuasive. So, I have a specific visualization for what I call my "Bad Coach." The Bad Coach is the one who just loves to talk me out of the great things I have planned. My positive voice, I call my "Good Coach."

In real life there are both styles of coaching. Just look at the football coaches in this country who have made the covers of magazines for their controversial coaching methods of intimidation, name calling, and other belittling behaviors. Personally, those types of cajoling methods never worked for me. I am always more motivated to do well when coached by my cheerleaders or Good Coaches. They encourage me! Give me ongoing pats on the back. Keep picking me back up after I trip and fall and say, "That's OK. Just keep going. *YOU CAN DO IT!*" Whenever I hear that positive voice in my head encouraging me, it's my Good Coach.

Whenever my Bad Coach sneaks in the picture, I have learned to be visual with him, too. I see myself grabbing him by the hand (or neck, whichever works best for you), and physically escorting him to my "OUT" door, and throwing him out at the same time I vigorously shout at him, "I don't have room for you in my life!"

There is also another way to use the power of words in your visualizations. Many people use "affirmations" as a motivator. Affirmations are positive statements about yourself and your goals, even if you have not yet attained them. Affirmations are written down, similar to goals, and might be worded like this, "I am a slim person," even though at this point you may not be as thin as you'd like to be. By repeating your affirmation to yourself each day you begin to train your unconscious mind into what you would like it to believe and to become.

However, with the role of visualizations, I prefer Anthony Robbins' use of what he calls "Incantations." He describes incantations as being similar to what Merlin, in the times of King Arthur, would recite to brave knights going into battle. Looking like he was in a trance, speaking with powerful forces from another world, Merlin might drone on and on in a monotonous tone, repeating, "You are the strongest knight in the kingdom. You are the strongest knight in the kingdom. You are invincible. You are invincible." Or any other statement that applied to each individual. Eventually, if the knight heard Merlin's chants often enough, he began to believe the message to be true.

One of the incantations I use when I workout is, "I feel great at 148!" Translation? I want to weigh 148 pounds and I'm programming my brain that 148 is the ideal weight for me! So I repeat to myself over and over, "I feel great at 148. I feel great at 148!" I must say it 200 times during my 20 minutes on the Stairmaster.

You can use incantations with your visualizations as well. If weight loss is your goal, you can visualize the new "thin" you doing physical things you hadn't been able to do for many years. You see yourself shopping, swimming, dancing, or any number of activities. You can also see yourself eating healthy and working out religiously. If on your weight loss journey, you always get hung up with French fries, try using this incantation, "French fries taste too greasy to me. French fries taste too greasy to me." Over and over and over again. Drill that new message and belief into your brain. You might be amazed at your reaction when you decide to eat French fries next time. You may still eat them, but your brain will keep telling you the message that you find French fries much too greasy. With enough persistence, you may start believing your internal messages and decide that French fries really don't taste quite as good as you thought. Voilà! Reverse

Your Powerful Weapons

brainwashing at its best!

So you see, visualizations can give you powerful ammunition to use in your battles. Don't just settle for the picture of the thin woman on your refrigerator when you can do so much more! Try various scenes in your movie and find which ones work best. Experiment with your words in your scenes to see which ones speak most powerfully. Using these three weapons together can be the overwhelming secret weapons your enemy isn't expecting!

One last story on how words have affected my life:

When I was a head nurse, I frequently went head-to-head with my supervisor who didn't seem to understand my concerns with staffing needs and various other issues in the unit. She frequently referred to me as a "Mack Truck," which was *not* meant as a compliment. I have held onto that negative connotation for years, wondering if my self-confidence came across too strongly, or if it was just her way of being my Bad Coach.

In contrast, a complete stranger helped me to change that negative image into one of positive power. When I was deciding whether or not to move to Cozumel for the winter, I made a quick five-day trip to the island to do some final research of the job market. A friend accompanied me, and on our return flight we were seated in aisle seats across from each other. Both of us are similarly built blonde women about 5'10" tall. The only major difference was that she had long hair and mine was very short.

As it was only three months after the tragedies of September 11, some passengers on the plane were still a bit unsettled about flying and were looking around for anything that provided them comfort. As my friend Deb was getting settled in her seat, a rather nervous woman sitting next to her breathed a huge sigh of relief. As Deb looked at the woman questioningly, the frightened passenger confided to her, "Oh, I feel much safer already." Pointing to me rather secretly, she added, "I'm sure that woman is a Sky Marshal!"

As Deb recounted the story to me later I was dumbfounded! What was it about me that made the woman think I was a Sky Marshal? Was it my confidence? (Little did she know I was still on the brink of depression.) Was it my new belief in myself and my purpose in life? (It had only been two weeks since my epiphany on the beach.) Or was I still so pissed off about being in the middle of a difficult divorce that I was giving off messages that said, "Don't mess with me?" I had no idea. What I did know was that the message I sent to that woman at that moment was one of comfort and safety, and that image feels much better to me than that of a Mack Truck. Thus, my self-concept now is as a "Sky Marshal" who exudes confidence, strength, passion, and wisdom, while at the same time creating safety and comfort in others. Talk about changing some negative brainwashing into positive! It doesn't get much better than that!

What image can you create for yourself that gives you strength, confidence and power? Be open to ideas that might come along. Decide what you would like to represent to yourself and others and design your own self-image based upon those thoughts. Just make sure you are a Sky Marshal and not a Mack Truck, and your image will work for you and not against you! So choose wisely.

"If you are working on something exciting that you really care about, you don't have to be pushed. The vision pulls you."

Steve Jobs

Chapter 21
Sabotage or Success?

So, you've decided now's the time for change. You have your plan of attack in place. You know the capability of your weapons and have them loaded and ready to use with the power set on full strength. Anything else you should know before you jump head-long in your battle with the boxxes? Oh, yes! There's still one very important piece to consider. Beware of saboteurs on your journey and keep your compass set only for success!

Sabotage

Have you ever noticed that when you finally make a decision to change something important in your life, it seems like everyone around you wants you to stay the same as you have always been? Maybe you've finally decided to quit smoking. You know it gives you bad breath, it is not healthy, and your kids are sick of your second-hand smoke. So, you've made the commitment. Bought your Nicoderm patches. Have a plan outlined.

Then, what happens? Your friends who still smoke show no remorse about offering you cigarettes, smoking in front of you, and basically, putting down your efforts to improve yourself. Perhaps they're even taking bets on how long before you're back with them in the "smoker's lounge." Why do they do this? This is one form of sabotage.

There are many reasons our friends, family, or even

strangers may try to sabotage our success — sometimes consciously and sometimes not. Basically, change can be threatening, and when someone rocks the boat by introducing change, there may be a ripple effect on others. They may think, "If you stop smoking, maybe you will think I should quit too and I really don't want to. Or what if I follow your lead but I fail? What then?" Instead of their inner self-talk saying, "I can't," saboteurs frequently turn it on you and say, "*YOU* can't!"

According to Dr. Phil McGraw in his book *Self Matters*, there are four types of saboteurs:

1) The "Overprotectors" try to keep you from failing and getting hurt. They don't believe in your abilities to begin with – usually because they fight their own self-esteem battles as well. They may really think they are protecting you when, in fact, they are slowly eating away at your self-esteem. Their type of sabotage involves trying to talk you out of your mission before you can ever start it. See if this sounds familiar: "Oh honey, I know you'd really be a great mayor for our little town. You're so kind and honest and caring. Everybody loves you. But how are you going to feel if you lose the election? Maybe it's best if you just let someone else take the job." Talk about mixed messages! Translation: "I love you. You're wonderful. But if you lose (and I believe you will) you might get hurt (which might also be a reflection upon me) and it's better to be safe than sorry." This is *not* a Good Coach! This is a covert, deadly Bad Coach sabotaging you. Beware!

2) "The Power Manipulators" want to keep you under their thumb. They enjoy having you depend on them and they fear a change in your relationship will threaten their own value as well. They enjoy being the experts or the parent figures wielding their authority over you as if you were a small child. It's all about them maintaining their power. For example, if

you go out with your girlfriends every week and suddenly you start doing something on your own, like taking Country-Western dance classes (which they don't want to do), they may begin to chastise you for your notions of what the class might do for you. While you might find it great exercise, a chance to meet new people, and are glad to know how to dance when you visit a Country bar, they might tell you how stupid Country music is, how only "hicks" hang out at those bars, and how those aren't "your kind of people." What are you thinking? That you might marry a cowboy? How ridiculous! Your friends are sabotaging you so you don't improve and leave them behind. Yet, they are too afraid to get Out of the Boxx and try something new themselves! Just ignore them and remember that you need to be true to yourself *first*, or you will be stuck in the boxx right along with them!

3) "The Levelers" don't want you to become better than they are and thus, try to keep you at their level or lower. They become jealous very easily if you find success in anything. This increases their underlying belief that they are not very valuable to begin with, and they will turn on you in a heartbeat. If they can't keep you down where they are, they don't want any part of you and will be glad to make your life as uncomfortable as possible. For example, let's assume you and a friend both work in the same company at the same level job. You decided to take extra classes so you can apply for a job requiring more skill and paying a better salary. Chances are your colleague will not be happy when you receive a promotion. Instead of being a true friend, joyful for your success, she will be spiteful, angry, hostile, and may threaten to break off your friendship entirely. You really discover who your unconditional friends are in these types of situations. Do not mourn her loss. Move on and find people who believe in you and leave the other one behind in her Victim Boxx!

4) "The Status Quo Seekers" hate the way things are but find the known safer than the unknown, no matter how miserable the known might be. Let's go back to your girlfriends who didn't want to take Country dance lessons. They may be miserable doing the same old thing every Friday night. They see the same faces and keep complaining "there just aren't any good men out there." They desperately want a relationship with someone. But they won't try anything new to see what possibilities might exist. So when you decide to take the classes, you invite them along, thinking they might see the benefit in finding new locations, new people, and new possibilities interesting and fun. Yet, despite their sad situation, they find the risk of taking a chance and thinking Outside the Boxx too frightening. The Fear of the Unknown Boxx has them locked in for life. Yet, they are not supportive when you step outside your comfort zone because you might just leave them behind. Don't let *their* Boxx of Fear hold you captive! Let them stagnate if they want. You can't live their lives for them, and you certainly can't change them.

I personally believe that there's one more type of saboteur . . .

5) "The Bully and/or Eternal Pessimist" is a person who may be a stranger to you but still finds a way to influence you in a negative way. Imagine that you are at the grocery store and decided to buy Nicoderm patches to begin your stop smoking campaign. As you hand your purchase to the clerk she turns to you and says, "Good luck. I know so many people who have tried these and they're still smoking. Seems to me it's a lot of good money for nothing!" Now you probably don't even know this person, yet how many times have you listened to someone like this and let their words hold power over you? Do you begin to doubt yourself? It's important to remember that people like this are generally negative about

everything. They simply like to bully people to feel more important themselves or else they just can't find anything in life to make them happy, so they sure don't want anyone else to be. Remember, you don't even know them so blow them off!

Sabotage can occur from without or within. It is wickedly underhanded and oftentimes quite hard to spot. It's easier to deal with when it's overt, but it can still be a tough fight. How do you do it to yourself? By allowing that nasty Bad Coach voice to come to the surface. Try some of these on for size:

"How can I try another diet? They always fail. This is a waste of my time. I just don't have the willpower."

"I'm just not smart enough to go to law school. Those lawyers have an IQ so much higher than mine. Who am I kidding?"

"I just don't think I want to risk getting hurt again. It's safer to stay home than try the dating game again. I'll just save myself the pain up front."

"I'm really hungry on this diet. This can't be healthy for me."

All these and more are the voices of the inner Bad Coach sabotaging you every single moment! Your power lies in knowing to anticipate it ahead of time and being prepared for it. Know it will creep up on you whenever you feel the slightest bit weak. Remember the OUT door in your visualization and get rid of the Bad Coach, no matter how many times it comes back!

On the other hand, you can't always throw out your friends and relatives who sabotage you, either covertly or overtly. Remember to use your arsenal of weapons against their attacks and stick to your course. It may be challenging at times, but remember that challenges only make you stronger!

Get Out of Your Boxx

Think of creative ways you can use your new Word Power and Commitment to show them who you really are. You might end up teaching them something along the way. Who knows? If they see you climb out of your boxx, perhaps some of them might gain the courage to climb out of theirs too. You could be a great mentor!

This past year I experienced many major changes in my life and was totally blindsided when some of my friends sabotaged me. When I returned from six months in Mexico, one of my closest friends met me with an onslaught of verbal abuse! You would have thought I had stolen her boyfriend, destroyed her business, and totaled her car, all in one fell swoop! (I did none of the above!) Some of her comments were:

"I know what you were doing down there. You were drunk on the beach all day."

"You got to go play all day while the rest of us had to stay here and be responsible and work for a living."

"Yeah, I know you believe you were suicidal last November, but what you really wanted was attention. It was all just a ploy."

I was totally confused, crushed, and dismayed that she was telling me how terrible I had been for leaving her while I went to take care of myself. Only now do I understand her behavior. She wanted to punish me because she hadn't been able to keep me in my boxx. Her sabotage attempts tied in to her need to be in control, as well as to keep me at or below her level. I didn't need her anymore and that upset her perception of how life should be. I didn't fit into the "niche" she had placed me in anymore. I had changed and the "new me" was threatening to her. Although it took me a couple of days to pick myself up from her scathing attack, I realized that the most important thing I had done was to be true to ME first and my friends and family second. She is no longer in my inner circle of friends and supporters. I recognized that she was not healthy for me and moved on to new friends who were more unconditionally accepting of me and were my cheerleaders, no matter what.

When you are assessing the direction you choose to take in your life, remember this: No one else walks in your shoes but you. No one else can understand what makes you tick, what life you live behind closed doors, or what fills you with passion. With that in mind, you must be true to *yourself* first and foremost. Your *true* supporters will be in your corner *with* you, whether they agree with you or not. Look for them and hold onto them tightly – they can help you through the tough times!

If you are ready to take a step outside your boxx, whatever step that may be, just know that there are saboteurs out there and they may be disguised as loved ones. You can choose to ignore them, keep them, or leave them behind, but know what your intention is and stick to it! Living Outside the Boxx is exciting but the path isn't always easy!

Success Strategies

Success strategies may help you reinforce your strength and armor and can be found in a multitude of avenues. One tool that helps me greatly is my "Success Team." We are a group of three women who have met almost weekly for the last six and a half years. We started out as just acquaintances who came together with specific goals for ourselves every week. We each took about 20 minutes to describe the previous week's successes as well as bumps in the road. We could then ask for help and/or clarification as to what we could do better, and then we committed to specific actions for the next week. The group would hold us accountable. Knowing that there was someone interested in our progress each week was exciting and powerful. We knew we could count on applause when that was appropriate. We also knew that team members would question our direction if we were not being true to our plans.

As the years went by, not only did we concentrate on our professional development, we became close friends as well. We have lived through a divorce, death of a spouse, loss of a job through bankruptcy, start up of two new businesses, one empty nest, and one "running away from home" episode! We cried on each other's shoulders, were our mutual cheerleaders, and celebrated wildly for each success we attained! We have grown personally through so many experiences, including being able to tell each other the truth, even when we didn't want to hear it. These women are my most avid supporters – both when I am up and when I am down. We email daily – sometimes several times a day. Even when I lived in Mexico for the winter and another of us wintered in San Diego, we were always there for each other and never missed a beat.

In addition to our supportive side, we know we will be honest with each other when it comes to important issues, and we tactfully approach situations with compassion and the knowledge that we can weather anything. We have had several "learning opportunities" (some might call them disagreements) and have come away from them with a stronger bond. This has been the most powerful group I have ever been a part of. We range in age from 47 to 61 and are so lucky to have found one another.

You can create your own Success Team. Seek out people who believe in success, growth, and the desire to improve themselves. You might have to go outside your usual circles of friends, the way we did. Even if you find just one other person, it's a good place to start. Weight Watchers and Alcoholics Anonymous have used this philosophy for years and the results have been phenomenal. So find someone who is on a mission similar to yours and help each other get there. Mind you, the members of my Success Team are all on different missions, yet our underlying theme remains the same: Growth, Support, Love, and Encourage, no matter what.

Another success strategy for me is to find a hero. There are so many great heroes to choose from. Any number of famous people come to mind. Oprah Winfrey has represented not only black women, but all women everywhere. She has diligently worked her way up in a predominately male world to become one of the most recognized and powerful women in America. Marilyn Van Derber, Miss America 1958, came out in the early 1990s as a survivor of incest, and has educated thousands of people about this horrific crime in an attempt to stop it. If sports figures speak to you, there are countless stories of "rags to riches" sports heroes who not only became famous and made vast sums of money, but who now work with charities to give back to their communities.

You may even find your hero in a fictional character. My personal hero is "Rocky" the heavyweight boxing underdog in Sylvester Stallone's famous movie. Rocky was a loser. He wasn't bright, good looking, hardworking, ambitious, or driven by money. Yet, when he was given a chance to fight the world champion heavyweight boxer, something so outlandish that it seemed impossible, he dug deep down within himself and became determined to give his best. He didn't even care about winning. He just wanted to hold his own against the champ. Despite the odds and the many saboteurs who would have him fail, he just kept plugging away and plugging away, day after day after day. No fanfare. No boasting. Not even many cheerleaders. Just a belief that if he gave of himself 100 percent, things would work out. He put his faith in God but took on the work for himself. And he persevered. He is my hero and he isn't even real.

I play Rocky theme songs in my car, especially when I am either on top of the world, or if I'm feeling a little bit low or apprehensive. I even took up kickboxing and love to beat the living stuffing out of my bag with punches and roundhouse kicks. It helps me let off steam while it fills me with a sense of power! (And it gives me some knowledge of self-defense at the same time.) I watch the Rocky movies every few months just to feel the huge sense of satisfaction that overpowers me at the end of each movie. I count on crying as the movie ends as I'm so filled with emotion. It is my re-energizing program. My positive brainwashing from yet another avenue. I feel invincible when I am Rocky.

Find yourself a hero. It doesn't matter who it is. Just find one and develop a relationship with that character. Be that person. Find their strength. Feel their successes. Acknowledge the qualities you have in common, even if the only similarity is a need to achieve your goals.

Use every success strategy you can find. But don't forget one thing. You still have to do the work. You can visualize yourself as a marathon runner winning the Olympics. Your superhero might be one of the great marathon runners of all time. You repeat your Incantations religiously each day and have the most detailed self-movie imaginable: seeing yourself receiving the gold medal at the Olympics, climbing up onto the winners' steps, hearing the National Anthem play, feeling the gold medal being placed upon you. But don't forget one thing. You still have to run and run and run to get your body in shape. You have to become strong. You have to go the distance. You have to know what time you will have to beat in order to win. You still have to do the work. No one can do it for you!

So when are you going to start?

"I smile at obstacles."

Tiger Woods

Chapter 22
It's Your Journey ...

When I was in college I worked as a movie projectionist for one of those now "old-time" movie theatres with only one screen. As a projectionist, I had to keep an eye on the screen periodically since things seemed to break down with certain regularity back then. Because of that job I have many fond memories of some wonderful movies: *Rocky, Star Wars, Jaws, Monty Python and the Holy Grail, Dirty Harry,* and *Butch Cassidy and the Sundance Kid,* to name but a few. What do these movies have to do with living Out of the Boxx?

Well, I'm a very visual person and I live through analogies. As I was developing this Boxx Philosophy, I kept trying to come up with analogies that might give people different ways to understand my message. Then I remembered my years of watching movies over and over. If I were ever to be involved in moviemaking, I knew I would not have been happy for long just being an actor. I wanted to be like Robert Redford, Clint Eastwood or Jodie Foster. I want to be the actor *and* the director.

The actors are told exactly what to say, how to say it, where and when to move, when to smile, when to frown, what clothes to wear and precisely every action, movement, emotion, and behavior to portray on camera. However, the actor/director gets the freedom and creativity to do everything *their* way! They get to decide all those things and more, including the lighting, what the colors are, and the pace of the film. They can change their minds and repeat the scene with a completely different scenario if the first one didn't turn out the way they liked. If they are producer as well, they probably even get to decide who will star in the production. They get so many more choices than those who just act, but at the same time they have so much more responsibility in how the film turns out.

Your journey in life is exactly that – YOURS! Each of us gets only one shot at life, whether you live to be 90 or only 20. LIFE IS NOT A DRESS REHERSAL! This is the only shot you get. With that in mind, who do you want to be – just the actor, or the actor/director? *Do you* want to let others dictate how your life will turn out, or *do you* want to make the decisions? *Do you* want to determine whether your sky is blue and filled with sunshine, or dark and stormy? *Do you* want to be the one who decides if the main character stands up for himself or lets those around him beat him into emotional submission? *Do you* want to play the character who is the eternal optimist, who finds joy in a variety of things in life, who faces challenges and sees them as character building? Or are you satisfied being told how to perform each step in your life — perhaps delegated to the role of the subservient, depressed, unhappy, treadmill-running robot? Or just a totally bored person doing the usual things that everybody else does day after day after day. Not a bad life, but not a great one either.

The choice is yours. Your life is YOUR journey and no one else's – unless you let someone else "boxx you" into the role of actor and not let you be the director too.

When you Get Out of the Boxx, YOU determine your life's direction. You make choices about which way your life goes. Of course, being responsible is still essential. The actor/director of any good film doesn't often make careless choices – he makes calculated ones. He does his homework to learn what he's facing. He chooses his scripts and actors care-

It's Your Journey

fully, gets a good handle on his budget, studies the possibilities for various locations, and then weighs the information well before moving forward. If he is a good director, he also reviews all of his old films and decides what things worked well and what didn't. He chooses his new direction from lessons well learned from his past. He doesn't stay in a rut with the "same old, same old stuff" or he won't stand out at the Academy Awards as something special.

You can do the same. I am not here to tell you to run away from home like I did. That particular Leap out of the Boxx worked for me at a time in my life when I didn't have to be accountable to a young family and I had the financial stability to take some risks. However, you can study your options carefully and decide how you can Get Out of Your Boxx in many other ways.

Examine your boxxes and ask yourself:

- ❏ Am I living the most exciting life possible? Can I make it better, and if so, how?
- ❏ Am I willing to take a responsible risk to make changes? What is the worst thing that might happen if I try something new and it doesn't work?
- ❏ Am I afraid of trying because I am afraid of success, of failure, of being criticized or laughed at?
- ❏ What if I fail? Would I be willing to try again, knowing that success frequently comes to those who are persistent? Or am I so fearful that I prefer to keep myself in a boxx that is limiting my potentials and possibilities simply because it seems safer, less time consuming, and requires a lot less work?

You don't have to be Nelson Mandela, Martin Luther King, or Helen Keller. It's certainly easy to rationalize that they were unique individuals with incredible inner fortitude.

Get Out of Your Boxx

Yet what about Rosa Parks? She was a humble, black seamstress in Alabama in 1955 who stood up for herself on a city bus during a time of segregation and refused to give up her seat to a white man. Her act of thinking "outside the boxx" ended up changing the course of a nation. As a result of her courage on that particular day, the future of Civil Rights in this country changed dramatically, and in 1999 she was awarded the Congressional Gold Medal. She was just an everyday, American woman who finally put her foot down and stopped living in the boxx that those around her believed she belonged in. She hurt no one by her action and took the responsibility for the reaction it caused. By standing up for herself and looking for the possibilities she might uncover, she changed history forever.

Your journey doesn't have to be so large that it changes history. Perhaps "Getting Out of Your Boxx" for you means finally summoning up your courage and asking for the promotion you deserve. You've done your homework and have other job possibilities up your sleeve if your boss doesn't value your work enough to pay you accordingly.

Or maybe it's standing up to your boyfriend and telling him you will be going out with your girlfriends every Friday night, despite the fact that he feels you should spend every free moment with him. (By setting good boundaries to take care of yourself, your relationship could actually become stronger in the long run.)

Perhaps it's standing up to your teenager and sticking to the punishment you threatened when she breaks the rules instead of giving in and minimizing the punishment when she complains that it's too severe.

Or maybe it's taking care of yourself for one week every year and going somewhere by yourself to rest, relax, recover, and listen to your inner voice help you get back on track. And doing so without guilt from what your family or others might say.

It's Your Journey

Remember that we are all on our own journey. We cannot truly walk in the shoes of another. We cannot change anyone else. We cannot *make* anyone else happy. But we CAN be true to ourselves and take care of ourselves first so that we can give back to others who are important in our lives. We can also decide exactly how we choose to respond to others with our attitudes, beliefs, and ability to look at things with an open mind. When we accept the fact that no one "made us feel" a certain way, we take responsibility for our actions and behaviors, and that responsibility gives us power.

Get Out of Your Boxx! Choose your own path. Don't let anyone else choose it for you. Just remember — don't let the carpool, your clients, or your spouse overwhelm you so that you lose yourself before you get all the way Out of Your Boxx! Make YOU a priority. You may be incredibly surprised at the possibilities you uncover along the way!

God speed and safe journey …

"There are some decisions in life that only you can make."   *Merle Shain*

Get Out of Your Boxx

More Out Of The Boxx Possibilities

If you enjoyed this book and would like to learn more about Out of the Boxx thinking, there are many possibilities from Out of the Boxx, Inc.

Keynote Speeches And Short Workshops

Mary Jo Fay gives keynote addresses and short workshops around the country. Ignite your conference with a one-hour or one-day workshop designed with your group in mind.

Weekend Seminars

For more in-depth study of your boxxes, our weekend retreats are offered at various sites throughout the country. Check our website for our current schedule, or we can arrange one at your location.

Power Out Of The Boxx Seminars

"Power Out of the Boxx" is a week-long seminar held in Cozumel, Mexico, most months of the year. This experiential retreat involves morning classes and group activities, plus a couple of evening events. Participants will be exposed to lectures, team-building, and the opportunity to step outside their boxxes with the many activities offered on this incredible, Caribbean island. There is still plenty of time for vacation fun! In addition, it may qualify as a personal growth expense on your taxes. (Check with your accountant.)

This seminar may be arranged at other locations.

For information on this and any other Out of the Boxx offerings, please see our web site at:**www.outoftheboxx.com**.

Please note there are TWO x's on Boxx, or you won't find us!

References

[i] Rape in America Study (1992) and National Center for Victims of Crime (2000).

[ii] National Institute of Mental Health and National Institute of Anorexia Nervosa and Associative Disorders.

[iii] National Institute of Mental Health